33 Short
Stories in a
Nutshell

CARLOS V. CORNEJO

authorHOUSE®

AuthorHouse™
1663 Liberty Drive
Bloomington, IN 47403
www.authorhouse.com
Phone: 1 (800) 839-8640

Published by AuthorHouse   03/04/2015

ISBN: 978-1-4969-7324-5 (sc)
ISBN: 978-1-4969-7325-2 (hc)
ISBN: 978-1-4969-7323-8 (e)

Library of Congress Control Number: 2015903288

Print information available on the last page.

TABLE OF CONTENTS

AUTHOR'S NOTE

So many hats we must wear in today's complex society! Even under a single hat or bonnet, our thoughts have to be thoughtful and fast-paced. I love the way our society functions and how determined we are to be part of the way it works. I also appreciate that many of us still can find comfort in personal, quiet time. For me and hopefully for you, reading is precious time.

The stories in this book allow us to forget about the hat we are wearing at the time we pick up a book and, instead, read about others' wearing their sombreros or mantillas in a fictional format. This is helpful because it breaks up demands imparted by routine or newly acquired tasks.

Since reading is such an individualistic endeavor of choice to achieve enjoyment and distraction, in the way that I view it, it is also the best selection to break into your day with new thoughts that are separate and take us away from what has been structured for us.

A book, such as "33 Short Stories In A Nutshell" is like having a friendly companion which distracts us from chores or the dwelling on more mundane callings.

Rethinking the plots of any of these stories may also add to your personal privacy. I say this because for me this was the case when I wrote these stories.

Carlos V Cornejo

Books by Carlos V Cornejo

Short Stories
    Different Coins in the Fountain, Volume I
    Different Coins in the Fountain Volume II

UNDER THE CATALPA TREE

After multiple placements in foster homes, twelve-year-old Roxanna landed at the home of Hazel and Horatio in the town of Albany. While there was only a slim chance that the Dvorak's could tolerate the outspoken, defiant, and rebellious nature of young Roxanna, they took a chance with succeeding in changing her behavior since, previously, they had luck with another youngster who stayed and became a member of their family. The newest Dvorak, Clementine, was now eighteen and living nearby with her grandparents, the father and mother of Hazel Dvorak.

The instant Roxanna was introduced to the Dvoraks, she asked what they did for entertainment in such a small berg of a town. Hazel told Roxanna that she would grow to like this nice town because good people had congregated here. She made it clear that people were sincerely nice unless they were given strong reasons for being otherwise.

The Dvorak home was ample, and Roxanna was given her own room. The school was within walking distance from her placement. Roxanna's private attitude was "that she was entitled to something better". Even Hazel and her husband seemed to be "sticks in the mud". In later conversations, she learned that they seemed to love boring endeavors as Bingo, bowling, gardening, and walking their German shepherd, Atticus. Roxanna asked herself, "How could persons under forty live in a sleepy place like Albany where the rush hour traffic consisted of only twelve cars traveling on Main Street"? Roxanna asked Hazel in her challenging voice,

"How else do you spend your time in this berg?"

"Child, we have many friends here. We visit each other every chance we have to get together. You'll be meeting them soon".

"Do they have kids my age?"

"Of course. You'll meet them very soon. We also have a great park to walk in and from there at night, you can see all the stars. The school you'll attend has a very good reputation and on Friday nights, there are sports games at the high school.

You'll soon meet my father and mother. They have a farm three miles from our house. Clementine is the name of our eighteen- year-old daughter who is staying with them in order to ride her black stallion, Towellger."

"What does Horatio do?"

"He sells and repairs farm and garden equipment at a former gasoline station on Main Street. He is very much in demand during this time of year".

Roxanna accessed all the rooms in the Dvorak house and viewed the large garden with rows of tomato, zucchini, eggplant, and corn planted along paths which led to a grassy area around a huge catalpa. In the meantime, Roxanna announced to Hazel that she didn't believe she was going to be in Albany for long. It just wasn't her kind of town.

"There is always a chance that you will learn that we are here to love you and root for you in the hope that you will learn to like the life that is here".

"I don't think so".

"Why are you so positive?" asked Hazel.

"You're isolated here. You probably just have one movie house, and I think you guys think playing checkers, Dominos, Monopoly, or Bingo is a great idea for having fun. That's not me".

"You have a point, Child. However, games that come in a box are meaningless unless you spend the game time warming each other's friendships. The gathering of friends in itself is enjoyable time. There is TV and radio if you want to look to the outside world for what is happening elsewhere".

The next day, a social worker came to the Dvorak's house with a folder in her tote bag. She had Roxanna's history and reports from the multiple schools she had attended in order to insure that Hazel and the school principal understand the lack of progress Roxanna had made in spite of possessing high intelligence. Roxanna was enrolled in the eighth grade at John Deere Public School. The principal hoped for the best. He thought there was a chance that she would want to adjust in this school which had very few disciplinary problems. Most of the children were bussed and strove to compete for top grades. Roxanna's first school week ended in two days, and during that time, she didn't see anybody who was capable of being her friend.

On Saturday, Roxanna climbed aboard Hazel's late model Ford pick-up to go to Hazel's parent's farm. Their arrival at the large Checkov ranch was where Roxanna saw a young lady in a large hat, checkered shirt, wide belt, and jeans.

"Is that Clementine?" Roxanna asked.

"That's her".

Mrs. Checkov hugged Hazel and knew better than to do more than welcome and shake Roxanna's hand. When Clementine came in, through the door, she surprised Roxanna by kissing her on the cheek and saying,

"Welcome, Sis".

Roxanna seemed to stiffen momentarily but immediately returned to a more relaxed mode when Clementine said,

"Sis, come. I'll show you around our nice little place".

Roxanna followed Clementine outdoors and was shown the chicken pen, rabbit hutches, pigeon coop, bee hives, and the small stable that was used for milking the family cow and housing two riding horses and a work horse.

"Could I ride one of the horses?" she asked.

"Do you know how to ride?" questioned Clementine.

"No, but I can do most everything".

"Then let's start you out on old Tony. He knows the farm and all the adjacent roads and trails. He is extremely gentle. He is the best for you until you learn to ride".

"I would rather not ride Tony. I'd like to ride the kind of horse that you ride".

"Okay, but you should hold on tightly to the saddle horn if you feel yourself going towards the ground".

When Marco started to trot, Roxanna felt herself sliding. Her feet left the stirrups and when she pulled hard on the reins, Marco abruptly stopped. She was going over the horse's head when she felt Clementine catch her in her grasp.

"This horse is wild" Roxanna exclaimed.

Clementine responded. "Tony is very tame and will keep his work pace so that you'll learn to ride in no time".

They returned to the stable and transferred Marco's riding gear to Tony. The girls rode about a quarter mile and stopped under another huge catalpa tree in order to get out of the sun and into the shade.

"Clem, did you know I am in foster care because my Mom wasn't good to me? I also have a half- sister who was also in foster care but was adopted by a family in Vermont seven years ago. I haven't heard from her since".

"Yes, my Mom told me. Do you know I was a foster child, too? Pop and Mom adopted me and now I am a Dvorak and am lucky also to have my grandparents who I love".

"I don't seem to be able to find whatever love is. Why do you think this is so"?

"What I have figured out for myself, Roxy, is that love is a growing feeling so complex that it takes time to have it get established. Relationships have to be nurtured and allowed to blossom. Love has its own time. It's not an automatic occurrence. Love is knowing who to trust. When we are little, most of us trust more people and things. As we get into adolescence, we tend to get more suspicious of adult motives. In the next phase of our development, most of us learn the importance of family and friends. In time, we leave our feeling of entitlement. We tread life more carefully.

Later in life, we change once again as we ourselves become young adults. In a way, we are like birds that get pushed out of the nest. Separated from their family, they become vulnerable to the survival challenges contained in the wider environment. You, like the birds, feel that you have been pushed out of your family and are now in the survival stage. But, unlike birds, you are not free to do what you want to take risks for your survival. During this time period, adolescents seek others of the same ilk to associate with because we are usually still limited in our learning capacity to think more broadly.

The time cycle we are in determines what we can give of ourselves. Life is not about taking. It's about giving. My father and mother gave me their love and at first I took it without cognitive thinking about what I was receiving from them. In time, they were giving me all the love they could. I learned that in returning love, I received more love. The majority of persons in town are givers. They share what they have and think. Takers usually hoard information and look to get the most of what they can from everything and everybody. They remain selfish beings and peripheral persons in and to what life is.

My Mom and Dad put up with me because they knew I didn't yet learn to appreciate what I was getting from them. Now, I truly love my family. They are givers and now I can say that I have grown to love the same bonding as they have. I know this because I have intellect and have learned many things by being so close to nature".

"Shall we return back home"?

The way Clementine explained that each person has to walk in his own continuum and to learn to love. Feelings have to be grasped and shared as we develop. This bonding helps us to be healthy.

On the way home, Roxanna asked Hazel if she visited her daughter and her parents often.

"Yes, I generally go to see them every weekend. When Horatio takes time off, we both go there and stay over. Sometimes, the three of us will stay at the ranch to complete the weekend. At times, we have also helped with harvesting of corn and in the baling of the hay".

"If we go to the ranch and they let me ride Marco, I might stay a while".

"That's nice. Roxy, maybe you also would like to stay because we all love you. I hope you know that we love you in a deeper manner".

The week went by and Roxanna didn't protest maintaining an orderly room and helping with the dinner dishes. She even took some interest in how an apple pie was brought into the world. On Saturday, Roxanna shared the family pick-up with Hazel and Horatio. At the ranch, she was ready for Clementine's kiss on the cheek and was able to give her a strong hug in return.

"Can we go riding today"? she asked Clementine.

"Sure. After today, you'll be ready to ride Marco".

"Can we go again to talk under our catalpa tree"?

"Yes, but first I want you to see the new day-old calf that Grandpa bought".

The calf was beautiful. It was a Hereford. Clementine took a milk bottle designed for nursing calves and let Roxanna feed the calf.

"See how dependent it is. We knew you were coming today, and our family agreed that you should give it its name. Is it a boy or a girl? Well, it will be more boy than girl as it grows."

Roxanna let that remark pass as she gave Goldfinger his breakfast. When they were under the shade of the catalpa tree, Roxanna stated,

"Do you like being on the farm and living in such a small town"?

"I love it"!

"Why"?

"My family is here and so are my roots. I guess I'm like the catalpa tree that was seeded here. It grew into a giant because it was in the right place. It found the soil and climate to be right for it to grow here".

"All that is good and well, but, are there boys here"?

"For me, yes. For you, the next few weeks will tell. There are large families throughout our valley. The families all know each other, and you'll be discovered in good time. Lots of guys are at college or working in their family farms. You will find out that we have great weekly hay rides throughout the summer, and dances on Thursday evenings. We have a two-week fair where you can enter Goldfinger when he is older. At the fair, you will meet many Four H'ers of your age.

As I told you the last time, it's not your best time for getting to know boys. Your time is right to think about having friends: some boys, some girls, but only in the form of friends. The most important goal should be allowing your roots to grow in place within the family. My childhood gave me the wrong roots. But, that changed when Mom and Pop gave me themselves. Now I'm so happy about who I am that I just don't think of wanting another kind of life. However, I told you that in time changes can happen that will invite other things to occur".

On their return to the ranch, Roxanna was confident that she had mastered riding Tony. It would be Marco for her the coming week. She gave Goldfinger his dinner and kissed him goodbye. On the way home, Roxanna told the Dvoraks,

"You know, Hazel, Clementine called me 'Sis'. Now I have the sister I always wanted."

"I guess she sees you as we do. You're part of our family".

When they arrived home, they found a note on their front door from Mrs. Whipple, the case social worker for Roxanna. She just wanted to see how everyone was getting along. She wanted to help if there were any concerns or problems.

"Hazel – I mean Mom, call her and tell her not to come. I don't like those kinds of busy-body people".

"I'll call her, but stay here because she is going to want to speak with you".

When contact was made with Mrs. Whipple, she had a list of questions to go over with Hazel and Roxanna. Roxanna's attitude seemed to return to what it was the last time she was in Mrs. Whipple's company. While Roxanna talked to Mrs. Whipple, Hazel slipped Rosanna a note to be more respectful. Mrs. Whipple's job was to verify that Roxanna was comfortable in her placement with the Dvoraks.

When Roxanna hung up the telephone, she asked Mom if there was some way to get rid of Mrs. Whipple and the other workers involved in her case.

"Probably, not immediately. We will see after a long while".

The school principal stopped in at Horatio's store and told him that contrary to all previous school records that were on file, Roxanna was surprising everyone by her current scholarship and behavior. He added that she seems to be hanging out with two other girls who were also very good students. When the next weekend arrived, Roxanna was most helpful getting the house in tip top shape so that they could all travel to the farm.

Upon arrival at the farm. Roxanna ran to the stable and found that Towellger and Marco were saddled and ready to travel. Clementine showed up and kissed her and received a bracing hug in return. They mounted up. Roxanna sat confidently on Marco as they made their way to the beautiful catalpa tree.

"Clem, I have been thinking about what you told me about when the time is right for roots to take place and how love can be a dominant factor in life. How did you get to find out about all that you know? How is it that you can think so clearly about yourself"?

Sis, you know that many emotions and thoughts make up each of us. There is an intuitive part in each of us that will play out. Faith is rather an important necessity to have in each of our tool boxes. It's part of our steering mechanism: the compass that determines the direction we will take and to which we steer ourselves. First, you have to have faith that you will have the motivation and passion to succeed. Then, people should be accepted for what comes out of their mouths until they give you reason to judge them otherwise. If you cannot have faith in friends, stop seeing them and steer yourself to spend time with your other acquaintances".

"Sis, you're so smart. No one else has ever talked to me like you do. You make a great deal of sense to me. How can I learn to be like you"?

Well, we have the same mother and father and grandparents, and they are truly responsible for what I have learned over the years by just being with them. What you can learn by listening and watching is as important as all the written knowledge that is stored in public libraries".

When they were back at the farm house, Roxanna went up to Hazel and hugged her. Then she hugged her new father and grandparents.

"I'm going to stay with you because you are my family. It's time for me to be your daughter.

I'm going to take care of Goldfinger. I'm certain he'll win a prize for us. I can't wait for the next County Fair!

LIVING ON A HOUSE BOAT

Jose Luis Estrada had lived on a permanently stationed flat bottom house boat in the estuary of the city all his life. He and his mother were together until Jose Luis graduated from college. Then, knowing that she was afflicted with rheumatism, she left her comfortable living to be with her brother in the dry air of Tucson. Jose Luis welcomed assuming his skipper-ship of his beloved house boat named "NoVa".

Jose Luis was not an ambitious man. He figured that his costs for living on the house boat didn't require him to practice his professional career. His bills didn't amount to much and for that, he didn't feel he needed to pursue his licensed vocation which was that of an attorney specializing in real estate. He was content to work as a custodian at a large hospital. He needed the exercise and doing the job efficiently allowed him to be relatively unsupervised. He liked working his 10:00 p.m. to 6:00 a.m. shift, cleaning, mopping and buffing the hallways. He didn't require much sleep and that was to his great advantage. He liked reading on the back porch that he added to the NoVa. It was only two feet above the bay waters.

For part of the day, he was visited by Picaro, a brown pelican that sat on NoVa's deck porch railing waiting for his supplement of cat food to be served to him. Picaro was nearly tame and allowed Jose Luis to scratch his head. A more occasional visitor that frequented the boat deck was Gusgo, a sea lion that shook himself dry so it could curl up to sleep there. He was befriended by "FBI", the pet rat terrier who resided on the NoVa. FBI got his name because he was always investigating everything and everybody that came aboard. FBI also stood guard when strangers walked on the floating quay to which all twenty-eight house boats were moored.

NoVa was in the middle of the fleet of house boats in the estuary. Seven feet on the left side resided Hussein Mowflin, a tall bearded and turbaned man who seemed to pray a lot. He was a good chess player and often invited Jose Luis to his house boat to play the cerebral game. Hussein was afraid of Picaro and never went aboard the NoVa. On the right of his houseboat was Haddie's boat and the NoVa. She loved to come and visit Jose Luis. Usually she brought his dinner and cooked it on his stove. FBI loved Haddie because he knew leftovers were going to come his way.

Haddie was not Jose Luis' love interest. She was too hippie and gypsy-like on the selection of her attire. Her great cleavage was easily viewed, exposing much skin when her unrestrained mega breasts were not restricted by an undergarment. Jose Luis felt that Haddie used her assets as a distraction to the fact that she was way over fifty. At the hospital, breasts were almost a daily exposure in some wards that the nurses did not monitor. Haddie's massive size jewelry was of more interest to Jose Luis than witnessing her heavily freckled upper body.

Haddie liked her booze and was well behaved when in the company of Jose Luis. When she went home and was alone, it was another matter. It was then that she drank her loneliness to invite sleep. Life in the estuary was neighborly and different from the conveniences of living on solid ground. On the house boat, the furniture was tacked down. The rolling motion of the NoVa made sleeping, TV viewing, and dining on moving plates, sometimes difficult.

One day, Hussein asked Jose Luis if he would lunch at a downtown restaurant where he had made reservations for Saturday. It was going to be his birthday, and he liked to have company on that day. If Jose Luis could have lunch with him, he could spend the night getting entertained by one of the ladies he had paid relations with in the past. She also had agreed to come to his boat for an elongated stay. For Hussein, sex was a problem only because he didn't drink alcoholic beverages.

The next day both men rode their bicycles to a famous restaurant which featured curtained booths. While the sourdough bread was being placed on the table, Hussein told Jose Luis that FBI was becoming aggressive because he probably didn't appreciate the turban worn on his head or the fact that he spoke his prayers aloud. Moments later, the maîtres'd and waiter returned to ask Hussein what was in the wrapped package he had next to him. Hussein became huffy and said,

"Why? Do you think it's full of explosives?"

"No, Sir, we are just vigilant because you have a turban and beard, and some of our customers heard some of the conversation you and your friend had".

Jose Luis said,

"Hussein, let's go to some other place".

As they were getting up, the waiter used his Cel phone to take photos.

"You guys are totally ridiculous" Jose Luis said.

"Please don't forget your package" were the last words said by several hovering waiters.

"I don't get you guys. We have done nothing wrong".

On that thought, Jose Luis said, "What's in your wrapped package"?

"Library books that I wrapped to carry on the bike's carry-on fender. I have to return the books on our way back home".

"What do you think the brouhaha at the restaurant was all about"?

"It's probably about my turban and the fact that your dog has a distinctive name".

"Oh, let's go into that place across the street and don't mention FBI".

On returning to the house boat enclave, firemen were in front of Haddie's boat. She was being carried out on a stretcher. It seemed that she had a heart attack or seizure. Jose Luis couldn't get any information. He, in turn, was being interviewed about what he knew about Haddie McCutchen. What an afternoon this day turned out to be!

Later he was waking up from his nap. FBI was in another uproar barking and barking. Two men were trying to board his boat. They identified themselves as FBI agents. Two others were boarding Hussein's boat. Jose Luis was asked to explain his friend at the restaurant and why they were suspiciously acting and mentioning the FBI. While Jose Luis gave them what explanation he could, he knew he wasn't too coherent. He knew that the FBI agents didn't believe his explanation.

As the FBI agents left his boat, Jose Luis looked out his door and saw his friend Hussein and a lady being taken away by the same agents from the FBI that were there earlier.

"Wait," Jose Luis called out!

"Buster, don't interfere. We know all about this woman and we want to know what's going on here. Listen, Jose, are you part of this illegal sex caper"?

"No, no, you guys have it all wrong. It's Hussein's birthday".

Two hours later, Hussein returned. He was extremely angry. Lady Lulu had been detained and he couldn't do anything about it.

Jose Luis couldn't sleep, so he went to work earlier than usual. He saw the white board that listed the names of all patients in the different wards. He noticed that Haddie McCutchen was listed in Ward 14B. He had time to look in on her.

"Jose, did you have a good dinner? I need you to take care of my house boat. Maybe FBI can be placed on guard in my boat while I'm laid up here".

"Don't worry, Haddie. I'll take care of everything".

The nurse came in and asked if Jose Luis knew the patient.

"Why, yes, she is my neighbor".

"Well, she needs to give us the names of her family members. Please see if she will disclose them to you".

Haddie knew that she was in jeopardy and that there was a possibility that she would not leave the hospital. Therefore, she told the nurse that she would give her the name of a family member.

"I only have one name to give you: Angelica McCutchen who is an RN at the city hospital in Oxnard".

Jose Luis kept thinking, "Oh, what a day this has been"!

The next day was peaceful. Gusgo was entertaining and kept the boat rocking with his prancing antics. Picaro was quiet after he had eaten the boxed take-outs from yesterday's birthday restaurant's luncheon.

Jose Luis went to the hospital at seven o'clock in order to visit Haddie before his shift started. When he arrived, the room was quiet. A young woman sat next to Haddie's bed reading a dated magazine.

"Hello, I'm Jose Luis Estrada, a friend of Haddie. Is she related to you"?

"Yes, she is my mom. I have been here all day. She is resting after the doctors ordered an angioplasty done on her. I managed to speak briefly with her. She's very weak. The medical prediction is that she will be okay and able to return home in a few days. I've been waiting for you because she told me that you could take me to her living quarters. She indicated it was impossible to find the place where she is living unless someone like yourself would show me the way".

"Glad to meet you. I'm surprised. I never knew Haddie had such a beautiful daughter. Let's go now since I have to be back at work by 10:00 p.m."

Jose Luis couldn't go home on his bicycle that he used to travel to work. He called a cab and showed Angelica Haddie's boat and the NoVa.

The next morning after she got over the shock that there was a sea lion and a pelican in residency on the house boat, she closed the door to the deck and returned to the kitchen. After introducing FBI to her, she asked if the dog could stay the night with her. The next morning, FBI woke him up with his barking.

"What you have is a zoo. I came over so we could have breakfast together. Mom has nothing to make breakfast with. So I'm helping myself to everything that you have in your refrigerator. I hope you don't mind. We are going to have hot cakes, Mexican papaya and coffee".

Jose Luis was surprised. At breakfast, there was a knock on the door. It was one of the agents from the FBI.

"Now, what"? Jose Luis thought.

"Who is this woman" they asked?

Angelica was sharp. She looked at Jose Luis and asked,

"Jose, are you a bad boy? Is that why the law is here"?

"No, no, I'm a responsible person".

The FBI man identified himself to Angelica and asked for her identification.

"Sorry to have bothered you, Miss" he said and left.

Angelica saw Jose Luis coloring to a shade of red and laughed.

"Angelica, this is not what you think. It's all Hussein's fault."

As he attempted to explain the presence of the FBI, he gave up and said,

"How could they think that this is a red light zone. It isn't. It's the most law abiding place in the entire city".

Angelica added that she didn't have to return to Oxnard for a few days. What should they do?

"Can you ride a boy's bike"? He asked.

They went next door to Hussein's to borrow his bike. His lady friend was there counting money and giving Hussein a kiss. Angelica teased Jose Luis by saying,

"Oh, I see that we have a difference in terms. You say this is the most peaceful, law- abiding place in the city, and now I'm suspicious of what the rest of this city is like".

"Angelica, get on your bike so I can show you this magnificent city".

A few days later, their next challenge was finding "a bicycle built for two".

THE HOUSE OF THE DAHLIAS

Chester was happy it was over. He had just walked his eldest daughter down the aisle and danced with her at the wedding reception. All four of his children and their spouses had been in attendance. Now he was chauffeuring each off-spring and spouses to the airport so that they could be back at their far away homes and ready to prepare themselves for work on Monday.

When Chester returned his rented tuxedo to the store, the clerk thanked him. Then, he called Chester back and told him that he had left a card in his pocket. The business card that he was handed was from a Charlise Towillisee. She was his daughter's best friend and the maid of honor at the wedding. It had a small note on the back of her real estate card. Chester didn't like Charlise much and thought slipping her business card into his tuxedo pocket was inappropriate.

When Chester went home, he sat himself on a patio swing that was in the back yard. He was surrounded by dahlias. His newly married daughter made it her hobby to cultivate prize-winning dahlias. That's how his Hanna met Cosmos, who was now her husband, a dahlia enthusiast. Chester looked at all the jumbo size flowers and asked himself what was to become of them. He only knew how to haul the manure, the compost, and enrich the soil in the yard. He didn't know tiddlywink of what to do with the prize bulbs or of filling out entry forms at the various flower shows.

As Chester contemplated the future of the dahlias, he knew that without proper care they would soon wilt. Dahlias required nourishing, water, and loving care. He only knew the part of giving them the required water. Besides, he thought it was time to do more for himself than to devote his life to do time consuming and compelling tasks in Hanna's ex-garden.

Chester guessed that Hanna had spoken to Charlise about his future. The house was too big, too much work, and too filled with his great memories of the past. Charlise must have thought that he needed to see her to be advised about down-sizing to a domicile that was more manageable for him in his senior years. After all, what were the chances that his entire family would ever come together again to visit. If they did, it would be when he was on his way out, or maybe too late for him to feast his eyes on any of them.

He called Charlise on the phone, and she answered in her nasal voice that irritated him.

"Charlise, this is Chester Sandoval. I'd like to talk with you about a couple of possible transactions that I'm bouncing about in my head. Perhaps you can tell me what the status of the housing market is? Is it a seller or a buyer's market? Can you come over and let me walk you through the house, so that you can react to the marketability of this house that has outgrown my needs"?

Charlise was nice enough. She was a long time, maybe twenty years friend of Hanna and sister Emma. Chester's two boys had never liked Charlise because she sounded as if she was talking through her nose. However, Hanna must of seen in Charlise what her real estate broker later saw. She was always distinguishing herself in the number of real estate transactions that she completed. She was the company's top money maker.

The day that Chester and Charlise met, she took nearly five hours to look around. She always took notes about everything. She had a fat guy walk around the house with his wheeled contraption that was used to determine square footage. When she took her leave, she told Chester that she would draft a plan for him that would spell out her best thinking. She told him that she was not going to take any commission because it wouldn't be right after all the kindnesses and business that the Sandoval family had given her.

When Charlise set up a formal follow-up date for them to meet at the "membership only" golf course restaurant, Chester was steered to a quiet outdoor table by the maître d'. Charlise told Chester that she had worked hard in developing her best idea for him.

"Chester, my plan is that you don't sell your great home. What I want you to consider is renting it to visiting groups which come to the city for cultural and entertainment purposes. We will rent only to visiting artists from the Opera, Ballet, Theatre, Symphony, and touring musical concerts, etc. This means we can rent your place for a high price for about 8 to 9 months of the year. We will hire a gardener, housekeeper, and maintenance crew to keep the property up to snuff.

Here is the other part of the package. My parents have told me about a house which is up for lease on their block. It's a beautiful three bedroom. You will need new furniture, but the advantage there is that we can lease that house for whatever amount of time you wish. The goal here is to have you keep your property because it will continue to appreciate. I also know that you may be wrong in thinking that your family will never come back unless the siren on an ambulance is blasting in order to hurry you to the hospital. How does this kind of program sound to you"?

"You're the expert. I like what I'm hearing".

Within three weeks, Charlise had hired the professional help needed to maximize the house by improving its new cosmetic look. She booked the management company that employed the gardener, housekeeper and maintenance personnel. She checked everything out with Chester on a daily basis.

"Chester, everything is ready to go as soon as we find a person who will chauffeur these important visitors around on demand. The vacancies left on the calendar are almost full because the De Colores Motion Picture Company wants to rent the house for seven months with an option for an additional two months. Claire Del Rio is walking away from her retirement and has signed up to be in for one last movie. She has one of the leading roles in another remake version of "Arsenic and Old Lace".

"Charlise, I loved watching Claire Del Rio in many movies. Listen, I'll be a chauffeur should you need one. My Lincoln Town Car is new and I can get myself that little cap that drivers use to drive special persons".

Charlise smiled, "Mr. Sandoval, remember that you have to assume the role of hired help. You cannot tell anyone you are the owner of your wonderful house".

Charlise called Chester two days later. "Claire Del Rio is already inhabiting your house. She is the first movie star to arrive. I have given her your telephone number if she should need a driver. Please answer the telephone calls by stating your name; otherwise, I may get a complaint. Okay"?

"Yes".

Several hours later, the phone rang and Chester knew that is would be Miss Del Rio.

"Hello, I have the day free, and I want to have an extensive tour of the city. Are you available and knowledgeable to help me get acquainted with this beautiful city"?

"Yes, Madam".

He was at his house in minutes. He was surprised that Miss Del Rio was ready. She wore an elegant suit. She was still a good looker. As Chester opened the rear car door for her to step into the car, she said,

"Look, I want to see the city. Please open the front door so I can sit next to you. I want to see where we are going. I know your name is Chester Sandoval, but if you don't mind, I'll call you Chester. Chester, I don't want to talk about me or any of the movies that I have been in. So please, let's start with a blank sheet and go from here. Capich"?

"Yes, Madam".

Chester drove her up and down the hills of the city, and explained the wealth of buried history that he could recall in order to enhance that which was seen in the various stops to provide detailed history. After a while, Miss Del Rio said she wished to be taken to a nice, quiet restaurant near the water. Chester knew just the place. Upon arrival at the picturesque restaurant, he opened her door and she looked at him.

"Are you going to leave the car double-parked, or what"?

"No, I know where to park it, and I'll be waiting at this spot when you are finished with lunch".

"Chester, I'm not eating lunch by myself. Go park the car and join me at my table".

What could Chester say other than "Yes, Madam".

The window seat had a wonderful view of fishing boats and sail boats on the well trafficked bay. While Chester worried that he didn't know if he should talk, or if he should talk about the sights that were outside their window, his mind was pondering subjects that could be suitable for conversation for a friend.

"What are you going to have"? asked Claire.

"It's the beginning of the crab season. For me, I would love to have their famous great crab salad".

"Wonderful! Please order two".

During the two-hour lunch, talk flowed as Claire managed to learn all about Chester's family and the fact that he was now semi-retired and had been an executive at the telephone company. After lunch, the tour of the city was continued for another couple of hours. He returned Miss Del Rio back to where she was staying. Before she departed, she asked,

"Chester, what's on the other side of the bay"?

The next morning, Miss Del Rio came out her door dressed in jeans and a checkered shirt and tennis shoes.

"Sorry, Chester, I should have called you and told you to come in casual attire. Why don't you take time to go to your house and change so we can have a picnic-type day".

Chester said,

"I can return in half an hour if you want me to change into more informal clothes".

"Nonsense, drive us to your house and I'll wait in the car. Then we'll cross the bridge and see the sights. Let's plan not to get back until we get tired. Are you up to it"?

The vineyards and small towns added light to Claire's big, brown eyes. Everything was so beautiful, and Chester steered the great car on the narrow country roads that fully showed off the splendor in nature.

When the rest of the movie stars began to arrive, Chester thought he had seen the last of his down-to-earth lady. He understood that there would be many locals and rehearsals in order to get the movie completed within budget and to meet their time constraints. When Chester didn't get a call in the morning, he thought he would call Charlise and see if she was free to have lunch. He never accomplished calling Charlise's number because Miss Del Rio called him.

"Chester, I'd like to ask you for a big favor. I need to read my lines aloud to someone. Would you allow me to rehearse at your house? It's too noisy where I'm at and I need a quieter environment. Maybe, you wouldn't mind listening to my lines".

Chester went to pick her up. She was dressed casually. He brought her to his house and Claire gave a set of the script to Chester so that he could follow her readings. To his and her amazement, Chester transposed himself and began reading the other actor's lines. Now they were both together on stage. Both read their lines with emotion.

Claire could tell that she was not going to have the heart to poison the old guy that Chester represented in the script. Claire looked longingly at Chester.

"Chester, I want you to call me Claire. You are my friend and now I can begin to tell you about myself. My real name is Claudia Ponce. I have been married three times and have no children. I am now surrounded by people who are not my friends. My main fault is that I expected a lot from people. I don't mind hard physical work. I like exercise, dance, good food, and love to keep house and make meals for my friends.

I live in Nice, Florida. I don't like my house and will be looking to move to this city as soon as I can make the arrangements. The movie I'm in now will be my last. You have shown me the way you deal with life and I want to stay close to you – that is, if you feel about me the way my heart is welcoming you".

"Claire, my heart is longing to be in your company. Now that I know I don't have to compete with your career, it changes things. We have a world of things to see and do".

Claire was in Chester's arms. Through the window, Charlise saw their embrace and passionate kissing. She decided not to ring the doorbell. Instead, she thought she had better have a talk with Chester. Her hard work in the weeks that she helped plan his real estate package, she never bargained that Chester would be much more than a chauffeur in the real estate caper that she had orchestrated. She thought trouble was ahead for Chester as it appears to her that he was abusing his role of chauffeur.

When Charlise set up a meeting with Chester to tell him of her annoyance, Chester remarked to Charlise that while he was grateful for all she had done for him, he had changed his thoughts about pursuing any further the leasing of his big house. He had other plans now. He told her that he would keep the gardener and maintenance personnel but that he would only need a house cleaner once in a while. He asked her to sit down. He told her that after the movie stars left for other ports of call, Claire and he would move back into his house.

"Charlise, you were right in telling me that someday there would be a good reason for all my family to return to my house.

The occasion will not be a funeral. Bells will be ringing in Claire's new dahlia garden".

MORAYA BENJAMIN

Moraya Benjamin loved spending her money from a great sum she inherited. Her aim was to enrich herself materially. Her mind was not to be super charitable or to fund worthwhile causes. It was to surround herself with the best that her money allowed her to buy.

Her passion was to experience making herself happy by obtaining something new and beautiful for herself. She shopped couture designers, hand crafted furniture, estate sale merchandise, hard-to-find original paintings, and the best materials available for window and floor coverings, etc. She relished going to auctions and art galleries to find accessories that she knew would show best in her mansion. She gathered her friends who devotedly applauded her newly found acquisitions. Her latest acquisition always gave her wonderful feelings of accomplishment and pride. The high that she achieved from her friends' accolades compared to that of a soprano in a major opera hitting all the notes correctly to receive the applause and a standing ovation.

Moraya lived for possessing beautiful things and the approval of others. She was a cultural elitist. A woman of exquisite taste. She liked to interject her self-styled refinement by using the specialized words that art critics and connoisseurs of art objects employed. She was something of a social gadfly and frequently invited persons to be in her company who appreciated her pursuits.

Her sleeping quarters were not only massive but also designed to the nine. The closets specialized in collections of about 400 shoes, 300 handbags and purses, 500 gowns, dresses and accessories. It was her plan to never be forgotten. When she would die, her future Benjamin legacy would be to donate the great mansion with the exquisite collections it contained to the city. Her bequest would insure that her fame would live on for decades.

For Moraya, living life with flourish was the ultimate priority. No concern was given to how narrow her ego seemed to those who knew better about what life really could and should be. In order for life to be more than carefree, it has to have some kind of objective pursuit – not limited to the acquisition of beautiful art. Moraya's world was perfect for her. Money would buy things and people. She also had health and a lot of time left to continue enlarging her art collection. She had what she wanted and needed. She thought she had life by the tail.

When the maid excitedly called out to Moraya,

"Miss Moraya, come quickly, there is a strange gentleman at the door who doesn't want to state his business with you. He put his foot in the door and demanded I bring you to him. Do you want me to call the police"?

"Let's go see what this is all about".

The stranger greeted her.

"Moraya, how beautiful you are. I know you may not remember me. You were only five when I last saw you".

"Sir, who are you"?

"Moraya, I'm your father".

"Sir, I want you to leave this house. My maid is calling the police".

"Police are really not necessary. If we sit down, I can explain why I am here – and I do have to be here.

Daughter, let me identify myself, and you will begin to understand that we are at a crossroad and are required to determine our next course of action. Moraya, this beautiful house was purchased by me. You have improved it and decorated it with great taste. However, what I need to tell you is that everything in your life is going to have to change. I didn't want strangers to tell you this. I am here to give you information and some bad financial news. Do you wish me to proceed or should we call your bank, CPA, or lawyer to verify that I am your father and that there is some very bad news you need to receive"?

"I see that your last name is Darby. That's not my last name".

"Moraya, when you were born, you were neither a Benjamin nor a Darby. You were born with my last name of Harrelson. I had your last name changed, as well as mine. There are reasons for that maneuver. Do you want to go into what happened twenty-one years ago, or hear the bad news"?

"Mr. Darby or Harrelson, I want you to tell me the truth because I don't believe you are my father. He died when I was five. My mother explained Dad's death to me".

"I heard your mom died. She was extremely embarrassed about my having to go to prison, and that's the reason for the change she made in your name. Benjamin was her maiden name. The FBI changed my name later when they placed me in the Protected Persons Program and saw to it that I was removed from you and the town. Moraya, the short of it is that I went to prison for nine years.

For twelve years, I have been running Synchem. That's a company that specializes in manufacturing synthetic diamonds. You see, dear, my mistake that sent me to prison was that my synthetic diamonds were sold in bulk as real diamonds. The money my company made was not reported, and, therefore, I also was charged with tax evasion.

That illegal supply of fabricated diamonds bought by the U.S. Government made us millionaires. It wasn't until they discovered that the diamonds they bought at high cost were synthetic that their discovery created a problem. The "Shit hit the fan". That's when they sentenced me to 30 years with time off for good behavior. Some Hong Kong gangsters also bought my diamonds and were out big money since they were cheated. They were on the look-out for me so that they could kill me.

After nine years, the gangsters who wanted to murder me were killed in their own gang wars. I returned to my company. We are a major manufacturer of synthetic diamonds. As chief chemist, my synthetic diamonds were so good that even professionals could not easily tell the difference between the real and the artificial.

After serving my prison sentence, I snuck back to my company and took my given name. I didn't dare come here to see you when the Pham Tong was hunting me. Now I am free to see you but I can't afford to buy this house for you. You must sell it in order for the government to recover its money, plus interest. Therefore, daughter, you have to move out. Now that the government has its records up to date, they know I'm alive, and they want what is owed them. Having given you title to this house when you were five years old has been judged to have been for the purpose of evasion and concealment. The government is aware of the fact that I purposely attempted to change the title on the house to hide it as an asset of mine.

"I'm calling my banker".

"Moraya, here is my newly printed card. Please take it. I'd love to hear from you. Please forgive me, Moraya. It's not as if we are totally broke. I still own Synchem. It's a profitable company. It is debt free. However, at the moment, I can't buy you all of the things that are here. All these wonderful things are to be sold at auction".

"Mr. Harrelson, I'm totally numbed by your explanations and shenanigans. I still don't believe that you could be my father. I can't begin to pull on my hair, cry and be in a panic in front of a stranger. So, please leave".

"I know, Child, and I'm so sorry. You don't have a lot of time to waste on emotionally distressing antics. We must plan what to do before the men who will be here in a week or two come in order to take inventory and appraise what is here".

"Mr. Harrelson, please tell me how to contact you should I need to see you. Again, I would appreciate it if you would now leave me to myself so I can verify what you have told me".

"Here is my business card, and I am staying at the Loyola Hotel. My direct telephone line is this".

He handed her his handwritten note paper.

As soon as Moraya had gotten over her shock and bewilderment which enveloped her, she began to think of how to minimize her losses. The first thing she did was to review the host of persons who came to her house and frequented her gatherings to dine and view her newest acquisitions. Moraya had her staff carefully pack her valued paintings which were considered to be masterpieces and substitute other ordinary prints at their wall spaces. She called her friend, the archbishop. Moraya was successful in making her appointment at the archdiocese.

"Archbishop, you have always admired the paintings I have brought with me. Now I have the opportunity to lend them to you so they can hang in your office for a year. Don't you worry about insuring them or anything like that. The paintings are only for your personal pleasure. I will need them back and hope you will approve this kind of loan".

Moraya went back to her house and had some ceramic Ming Dynasty and French pieces placed in the basement. She had a ceramic repair professional superficially impose lines which gave the appearance of small fissures on all of the fragile pieces. The lines could hopefully be removed by the same craftsmen at a later date. The teams of personnel who took inventory and the certified appraisers estimated the value of each item. Their job was finished within three weeks. Moraya was given copies of what had been recorded for the purpose of determining what was available for the government to recover the financial losses they sustained years ago.

The mansion and the carefully designed landscape were estimated to be worth 23 million. The total contents of her furnishings with the exception of the make-believe damaged items in the basement, came in at 62 million dollars. The total was 85 million, or about 10 million more than was owed to the government. Moraya smiled to herself because the government would owe her 10 million. If she sold her art masterpieces, she could buy everything back by herself. Seventy-five million was about the worth of a small painting she stored at the archdiocese. It was thought to have been painted by Sanzio Raphael.

It pained Moraya to lose any of the things she had and loved. They were like an extension of herself. There had to be another way of allowing esteem to return to her soul. She felt strongly that she had to be in the company of beautiful things. To have something that was hers taken away from her, wounded her. She started to do research on people. She started with her friends. She needed new friends that could be of greater help to her in situations, such as the current ones. Her team of researchers worked eight-hour days and compiled a short list of people to add to her friends who frequented her display of acquisitions. The question she attempted to resolve was who could allow her to regain most of what she considered to be hers.

In the meantime, she called Mr. Harrelson to schedule a meeting with him. He was at one of his offices in Antwerp. He told his daughter that he would be going back to the Loyola Hotel in a couple of days, and they could meet then.

"Father – I know you are my father because I'm just like you. I, too, like money. I, too, will resort to illegal doings to retain what's mine. I'm sorry I mistreated you as you have mistreated me by allowing me to believe that you were dead. It was terrible not to have a father after I was five. I now have to get us together, and now you have to be my father and support me".

"Moraya, just let me be in your company for short periods of time. You'll find out about the love I have stored all these years and that emotion remains deep within me. I'll prove my love for you if you let me into your heart".

"Father, I don't have to leave my house until it is placed in the market place. Do you know that the government wants their 75 million from the sale of this house and all the furnishings? The house is worth 23 million. The furnishings bring the total to 85 million. The government is going to owe me 10 million, if they sell all my possessions".

"Moraya, I can have about 10 million when I sell stock in my company. You can have that if you need it".

"Father, I need it. Why don't you leave your hotel and come and stay at my house"?

Moraya had her mind set to retain her house through negotiations with the involved government agencies. She was about 3 million short of the asking sum for her house. All she had to do was figure how to pay back a loan of that magnitude and she could start buying additional pieces in the years to come.

One day, Moraya sat down at the breakfast table and happily told her father that she once again owned her house. The next item that she told her father was that she was having a party on Sunday.

"Father, you must come. You will love what I have in store".

On Sunday, her new and old friends were standing or seated in the grand ballroom when Moraya interrupted festivities and addressed the cheerful group.

"I want everyone here to meet my father. He has been away for 21 years. But he is here now and my life has changed for the better. I also want Tex Laughlin to come and stand next to me".

A muscular, handsome young man of about forty left the couch he was sitting upon and stood next to Moraya. He held her hand and gave her a peck on the cheek.

"Tex and I were married on his enormous ranch weeks ago. He is coming to live here, and I want everyone here to get to meet him. He is a Yale man. He is well known and sits on the board of the Metropolitan Art Museum".

Her father was flabbergasted. He shook Tex's hand and gave him a hug. Her father told Tex that he was welcomed into the family. He congratulated both his daughter and him.

Then, her father pulled on his daughter's arm and escorted her to the study. He closed the door and said,

"Moraya, tell me, what's the mystery"?

"No mystery, I researched him. I negotiated where we need to live. I found out everything about him. He has all the money that we will need. I even know his DNA; I shopped hard to get him. He is truly the best, most refined person available. I looked up other persons who had more wealth. However, he has the looks, chemistry, and hormones that are exquisite. He is a rare man, and he has never been married. He is a real connoisseur and will be a wonderful asset to me.

I told you, Father, we are very much alike. I think I am craftier than you because I'm going to skip going to prison. At this moment, I have more than what I had before you announced the debt owed to the government".

"I guess you didn't take after your mother after all"!

A PIECE OF WORK

"I don't see what Ruby saw in that old man of hers.

How is it that such a gorgeous lady who must have had suitor after suitor in her life get married to a Ben?

You'd think he was a millionaire or world traveler with great adventures to relate. My understanding is that he is well off but not the kind of tycoon that Ruby could have landed for herself when she was in her prime. She still is a knock-out in her looks. I'd give her a 9-1/2 out of 10 on the beauty chart".

"I agree with you. My take is that Ben doesn't seem to have the personality or social connection to foster happiness in another person. Yet, Ruby seems so happy, always smiling, laughing, and sparkling the friendships we have with her."

"Jack, what if we try and solve the mystery of how those two met and how they have endured the seven years that Ruby says she has been married to Ben".

"Joel, this would be an interesting project for us. How does a guy with run-of-the mill looks, driving a three year old Nissan, who seemingly has ordinary resources, get a gal like Ruby to marry him? He certainly doesn't seem to merit a trophy wife. What do we really know about Ben?"

"I have an idea. Why don't we get close to them. Let's invite them to dinner. Can we spruce up your house and ask them for a convenient date so that we can welcome them to the neighborhood? Maybe a little dinner talk will help clear up how that old guy married the most head-turning gal in this town. He must be twenty or more years older than Ruby".

Since Ruby's hours to go to her fitness club conflicted with the normal hours that people sit down to dinner, she declined their dinner invitation. She purposely loved going to the gym when there were only a few dedicated persons there during the 5 to 8 p.m. hours. Joel managed to arrange an afternoon lunch at the club house of his private golf club. Joel and Jack, Ben, and Joel's lady friend Melissa, decided to share in the process to secretly probe the background which connected the Wilkersons with each other. Melissa was also acquainted with Ruby and admired the way she comported herself and greeted everyone with twinkling eyes, a smile, and genuine warmth. She had met Ben once, and, like Jack and Joel, it was her thought that Ruby and Ben didn't go together. What was Ruby's attraction to such an ordinary and older fellow?

In lieu of a dinner, lunch was set at the golf course where its dining room overlooked an elegant landscape. The club house's tables were richly decorated. The only problem was that there were many persons dining there and the noise level prevented great conversations from taking place. During the eating of the entrée, Melissa stated.

"You two are such interesting persons. How did you happen to come to our fair city?"

Ruby responded,

"We did our homework and loved what we read about this city. So we packed up, came here, and never looked back".

"What city did you live in prior to coming here?"

"Our stay before we arrived here was Atlanta".

Ben posed the question,

"Who is the golfer? Do all of you come here often?"

Before the question was answered, a large party of guests arrived to celebrate a young man who was getting married the next day. The all-male contingency added to everyone else's discomfort. So much so that the further probing to secure the information that they desired had to be put on hold.

After the Wilkerson's left, Melissa indicated that they mishandled the entire probe. Their strategy should have been better executed. Now the plan was to attain more particulars about what seemed to be a bi-polar or paradoxical marriage? What to do next?

After a round of martinis, it was decided by Jack and Joel that Melissa should join the fitness gym and be there during the hours that Ruby indicated were calendared for her to exercise. Joel and Jack agreed to buy her the required membership. Two weeks later, Melissa was at the gym at 3:30 p.m. so that she could be there prior to Ruby's arrival.

"Melissa, I didn't know you were a member here. I've been coming here about four months and never bumped into you. Strange, isn't it?"

"Ruby, I have just decided that I needed to tighten my buttocks. I'm afraid I was going to inherit and replicate my mother's derriere. What piece of equipment would you suggest that I use to lose my unwanted fat? Should I just work out on that stationary bike?"

"Every movement of your legs and abdominal muscles will help. The main thing is that every day you add one minute to your routine. Anyway, ask Morris for some help. He'll be here at 7:00 p.m. He is really good. He also keeps his hands to himself. Well, so long, I'm going downstairs to the sauna".

"Would you mind if I tagged along?"

"Not at all".

No one was using the women's sauna. The two ladies had the benches all to themselves. Ruby set the timer so that they would not over-stay or relax to the point of dozing off and endangering themselves.

Melissa could hardly breathe. She didn't like the dry heat. Her body was totally wet. So Ruby told her to remove her towels. Melissa was hesitant but did so. So did Ruby. Once again, Melissa was overwhelmed by the perfect proportions that she witnessed in Ruby's totally athletic body. How old was this super specimen of her own gender?

In such conditions, talking was not for Melissa. They left the sauna within fourteen minutes. They hydrated themselves and sauntered back to the gym. Melisssa said,

"Ruby, I'm twenty-six. How old are you?"

"I'm thirty-something, but I don't want people to peg my age. When we advance a bit into being better friends, I will tell you what only my mother and husband now know about me".

Melissa went from the gym to her bed. She did not answer her phone and slept like a baby until her alarm clock rattled the silence in her studio apartment. Then, she dragged her aching body to the real estate office where she worked.

Melissa expressed to Joel that she thought Ruby had a good marriage and was just a wonderful person. Furthermore, she thought they should forget being private detectives and go on to more constructive endeavors. On the other hand, Joel replied that they were not interested in stirring up anything of an unsavory nature. They were just kind of wanting to know how the Wilkerson's kind of romance ticked. He himself wanted to know how did an unattractive guy who is nearly twice the age of a beautiful lady get her to be a wife???

"You have met Ben. He is not in a power position or have big money or have a handsome appearance".

Melissa continued meeting Ruby on a regular basis. After work, Melissa went to the gym and met Ruby at the juice bar. They talked about all subjects. They became fond of each other. One day, Ruby reached to hold Melissa's hand and asked,

"Melissa, when we first met, why did you ask me how old I was?"

With Ruby still holding onto Melissa's shaking hand, Melissa told her,

"Ruby, you'll think I'm a terrible person when I tell you about the reason for asking your age. You don't know how catty Jack, Joel, and I can be. Ever since you arrived in our town, we have speculated that the difference in age between your husband and yourself doesn't make sense on the surface and that there must be some unknown reason below the surface to explain your devotion to each other. The three of us were simply sticking our noses into finding out what we could learn about your age difference and the personality differences between you and Ben.

I'm so sorry that I was made part of their scheme. I can assure you that I have not been telling them anything you confidentially discussed with me. I have too much respect for you. I plan to keep my nose to the ground. I'm not certain that I will continue being friends with them. You see, I have grown to like you so much that I consider you to be my best friend. NOW, you know. I'm not the good person that you thought me to be. Ruby, I do think the world of you. I will not make another mistake like this one."

The whole time Melissa talked, she cried and the wetness of her tears were continually transferred to her handkerchief. When Melissa concluded, Ruby sat still for about three minutes and made no attempt to console Melissa. Then, she refilled their glasses with fresh vegetable juice.

"Melissa, Ben and I do want to keep our lives private. We have attempted to keep my secret from surfacing and not add complications to our new lives in this, our new beginning. Ruby, Ben and I are only four years apart in age. Melissa, do you have time for my story?"

"Ruby, I don't need to know anything about you because you are already my hero. I just want to stay friends with you".

"Thanks, that's a great answer. Now I know that I can tell you a little more about myself. I don't believe I could ever tell anyone else that I have met about the last eight and a half years of my relationship with Ben. We have been married for seven years, but we have known each other for more than eight.

Before actually meeting Ben, I had read about Ben Wilkerson in several magazines. When I became interested in making an appointment with him, I investigated him by looking him up in the internet. At his office, I was shown examples of his work. When I met him, I told him that I had saved twenty thousand dollars that I could spend on myself. That was all the savings that I had. He looked me over and gave me an appointment. He fixed my cheeks, my eyes, ears, and my forehead and chin. The results were so sensational that he insisted on continuing on a pro bono basis by doing my neck. After that my belly, boobs, calfs and thighs.

Ben saved me. He enhanced my self-esteem so that I am much happier. I am a different, more gorgeous person from head to toe. He remade all of me within the year and a half that I went to him. He told me that my body did its part because I was a remarkable healer and had the right type of skin. I was his best piece of work. He told me that I would remain perfect only with the right kind of touch ups, and an exercise regimen. Ben has stop working because he has been free of suits, and we have enough money to play for a long time. We have no children even though he could have arranged that, too. We are happy. He loves me because he has made me what I am. He's still the same great guy. I don't see his age because if I did, I would have to re-think how I would have looked without Ben."

After promising to always be friends, Melissa left the gym.

That evening, Joel called her and asked her if there was anything new from the gym. She gave him a loud "NO! I am not going to betray my friend."

Then she added,

"Jack and you, Joel, can drop dead. If and when you guys grow up, send me a note. I now have more maturity. If you guys get to that place, too, we'll be friends again".

BROTHERS

Chris Harrington, Albert Jordan, Billy O'Brien, and Horacio Sanchez grew up as if they had been brothers.

They attended the same neighborhood parochial school for nine years and stayed together for three years at a public academic high school.

The congressional war hawks been voted out of office by the late 1940's and our nation was at peace. Then High School graduation was over, the four life-long friends remained in the community. Chris became a policeman; Albert a fireman; Billy's parents provided funds to open up a refrigeration repair shop; and Horacio committed to continue his education at the seminary.

Whenever they could, they met at the Rusty Kettle for conversation over a few beers and corn beef and cabbage and potatoes. Their lives were ordered and uncomplicated. They grew up without the need to join gangs, be influenced by the demonstrations of rabble-rousers and, basically, adhering to cherished linear thoughts and ideas. The goals they set for themselves were sequential and provided satisfaction to their families.

For each one of them, other than Horacio, looking for the right girl was made difficult because of their mixed job schedules. When they gathered at the Rusty Kettle, it was to focus and renew experiences. Horatio listened but, outside of laughing at their various pursuits to meet girls dances, church, movies, restaurants, picnics, parties, and have parked car episodes, he thought that what he heard was ungoverned hormones at work and perfectly normal for his friends. When Horatio had embraced his universal church, Chris, Albert, and Billy were proud of his committed vision to help steer common sense and righteousness on the world stage.

What was unchanged in Father Horatio was his continued attendance at the Rusty Kettle to meet with his three adopted brothers. It was most important for Horacio to have his extended family be in contact with him and to discuss interests and thoughts together.

While Horacio was an excellent thinker and orator, he curbed his own skills to allow for his brothers' egos to be heard and not be interrupted or dampened. He considered himself fortunate to have been assigned the parish he attended for most of his life. Now, he was most needed because the monsignor had a secret addiction and could not perform many of the public duties. He had to rely on Father Horacio, who knew the community well, for many of the ecclesiastical responsibilities outside of the church.

On a scheduled Friday evening at the Rusty Kettle, the three "musketeers" and he (D'Artagnan) met to chat, let their hair down, and speak the newsy items of their lives in police work, fire problems, and the housing demands for bigger and better refrigerators. The talk about obituaries, marriages, orphans, and church financing was usually left for last. On this last meeting, Horatio was eager to provide his good news. He cautioned them that what he was about to tell them must be kept within their inner circle.

He explained that Bernard McCarty II died and left their parish two million dollars which he willed to St. Mary's church. He also willed the church a small privately owned island in the Caribbean that had been abandoned years ago when it was last used as a residence for recovering alcoholic priests. He described the island as having two big structures and the island could be reached by boat from Puerto Rico in less than two hours. The island has great beaches and was a fisherman's paradise.

All three of his listeners were intrigued and reacted with their individual fantasies. Their thoughts surfaced in their questions. Albert was the first to ask,

"What would I do on a holiday on that island"!

"What would you do besides fish"? asked Chris.

"I would ask my girlfriend to go with me and that would augment whatever pleasurable world exists there. You know how Maggie is always claiming home harassment and worrying about her lack of privacy in her house with eight brothers and sisters. I know she would love it there".

"That's a great idea, Al. I would ask Janice to go with me. She might want to take Shuck-Up, her ten-breed dog. We'd all have a ball. Just imagine: no telephones, long warm summer days that I presume great sunrises and sunsets that might get her in the mood to cuddle ourselves with each other".

"Chris, you and Al are dreamers. I'd take five cans of insect repellent and lots of sun screen. Who knows, there may be sharks near the beach. Don't get me wrong, I will not go with Alice, until I know what the place is like. I'd go there with the three of you and no one else."

Father Horacio interrupted, "Billy, I think your idea of not inviting the ladies at this time is a good one because that island has been deserted from way before the war in Europe. The monsignor and I need the three of you to go and give us your assessment of what the St. Mary's community should do with such a property. The monsignor and I trust you fellows. I can't go because he is dependent on me to maintain the various commitments in which we are currently involved".

Billy and his brother companions understood the underlying reasons. Chris spoke up for the three,

"Okay, let the three of us go. Let's take vacation time and fly to Puerto Rico and charter a boat to get there".

Synchronizing their vacation took a month to schedule. Father Horacio asked them to take his camera to snap photos as needed to tell the story of what was on the island. They took a detailed nautical map as to where this island was located. They also took insect repellent, sun screen, the standard medication along with a first aid kit recommended for travel in the tropics. They made advance reservations with a Puerto Rican captain owning a small private yacht. The name and address of the captain had been provided by a monsignor-friend. Chris, Al and Bill met with Captain Sandoval. To the surprise of the mainland Americans, the yacht was great and had ample sleeping facilities.

Captain Sandoval looked at the nautical map and questioned all of them as to the certainty of the location. They presented copies of the deed to verify the location. The captain shook his head and said that he was willing to learn and be surprised as to the unnamed and poorly marked rock to which they would be sailing. The location seemed to be near a well-known island.

As an island came into view, it looked larger than they had been led to believe. There seemed to be human activity and a large building. The coordinates checked out. It WAS the church's island. When they came onto the beach, there was a small pier to tie down the boat. A rather large building had a sign that read "Bilmont Hotel" on its façade. The three musketeers thought that this was not the place that had been described to them. They were expecting a deserted rock or coral island with two abandoned buildings and some "no trespassing, private property" signs posted everywhere.

They persuaded Captain Sandoval to circle the island about three miles out in order to satisfy themselves that there was no other island in the vicinity. They needed to assure themselves that they had come to the correct island. Although the sky was clear with good visibility, there was no other rock or coral island at the location provided by their multitude of documents. They agreed that the best thing to do was to go ashore and document everything that they saw. They took photos of the hotel, its large propane tanks, generators, and refrigeration and air conditioning units. They photographed the beach, topless ladies, beach furniture, sports equipment, and the numerous boats tied down to buoys near the pier.

After recording all they could, they discovered that the hotel charged $450.00 per single room per night and that the restaurant and bar at the reserved sea water swimming pool also had what seemed to them to be outrageous prices. When the three were satisfied that they had accomplished their goal, they were ready to return home. In their hearts they felt that they had been on a wild goose chase. They decided not to call Horacio from Puerto Rico because their photos would tell it all. Armed with the photos and Captain Sandoval's signed statement that the island they went to was at the coordinates provided him, they returned to Pittsburg and made a bee line to meet Horacio at the Rusty Kettle.

At that meeting, they presented their case based on their thinking that there had been a "joke" played on the church. However, Father Horacio said,

"Not so. The church definitely owns that island. Remember that Mr. McCarty allowed the island to be used to treat priests for years, and you saw it as being abandoned because of the expense to the church".

Father Horatio realized that he must go personally to the island. He would need to go with resources available at the church. The church's legal staff would straighten the problem that existed. In the end, the courts would have to decide to whom the island belonged. Four months later, the monsignor and Father Horacio had the information that convinced them that the church owned that specific island. The Biltmont Hotel owners must have illegally appropriated that abandoned island without the benefit of a title search. The legal case took over a year to sort out the myriad details contained regarding ownership.

A legal resolution was agreed upon by all parties. While the church owned the island property, it could not claim ownership for the improvements that had been made. Therefore, the hotel would have to be given a long-term lease. The church had the responsibility to bear the costs of any additional improvements and it was to be paid $40,000 U.S. dollars per month by the lease for the next seven years. Taxes would be paid on the business transactions because the island was not a part of the USA. Therefore the church property was not tax exempt.

The monsignor called a meeting at his parish residence for Chris, Albert, and Billy and Father Horacio. At the meeting, he spoke of the good news that the church could report about the agreement made with the island tenants. He spoke of the great sum being provided the church and told the three parishioners that he was appointing each of them to be on the church's board of directors. That would entitle them to visit the island twice a year for a week at church expense. If they married, they would also be able to take their wives and family but not their "girl friends". Father Horacio smiled and added that in the future each of his brothers, family included, could synchronize schedules and meet on the island in lieu of the Rusty Kettle

The second year, the musketeer brothers, "One for all, all for one" managed to go on a fishing trip to the island. Father Horacio remained behind. They rented a late model eighteen-foot Chris craft. Two miles out from the far side of the church's island, the fellows decided that two of them should take turns in the water snorkeling. One of them would always remain aboard the anchored boat. Billy was quite a good snorkeler and wanted to dive to the seemingly shallow bottom. He did this because he thought he had seen some unusual formations below the boat. Diving down with a rope tied around his waist, he found that the sea bottom contained ruins of buildings. He saw a metal piece with an iron pipe attached to it. He removed the rope from his waist to secure the intriguing metal piece. He guided himself up the rope and asked Al and Chris to pull up the rope. With the three of them looking at what their catch had pulled up, it proved to be an almost unreadable sign.

Using some gasoline to clean its surface, the faint letters began to be deciphered. What they had discovered proved to be a sign that read: "No Trespassing – Private Property". "Could it just be that this sign was discarded by the Hotel folks? Billy asked.

"Tie me up. I'm going down again. He went into the sea with an oxygen tank on his back. As he swam, he saw the foundation and debris that appeared to be remnants of two large buildings, together with other posted signs similar to the one that had been pulled up. The shallow sea floor seemed to be composed of powdered coral.

As soon as Billy was back aboard the fishing boat, the three bosom friends gathered to hear what was discovered. They began to suppose that perhaps what was beneath the surface of the water was originally the island that they were charged to find. It could be that the church's coral island was twelve feet underwater. Had there been an earthquake or some oceanic disturbance that had collapsed and sunk the church's coral island? When, how, and why had this happened? They surmised that the judge who tried the case had given an incorrect verdict. As far as they were concerned, the evidence was plain to see. Talking amongst themselves, they decided not to disclose their findings. They would report back to the monsignor, especially since he was paying for their fishing and swimming vacation.

On their return home, they called Horacio. He expressed his disappointment and said that they should meet and discuss their thoughts with the monsignor. At the meeting, the monsignor indicated that he needed time to ponder his course of action and asked that everyone return in three weeks. This would give him time to consult with the church's legal staff. The churches finances had to be reviewed and the effects of any lost revenue had to be re-calculated.

In the meantime, the four met at the Rusty Kettle to continue pondering the strange situation of an island that crumpled into the sea. The three who made the underwater discoveries leaned to the fixation that a big mistake was made in identifying the wrong island as the church's property. Luck and glee had turned to disappointment. Father Horacio was the most troubled. He didn't like knowing what he now accepted to be a humongous piece of bad news for his church.

The time to meet with the monsignor finally arrived. The monsignor looked at everyone and saw the troubled look upon their faces. He and an attorney told their small audience of four that the case had been argued in court and a correct verdict had been rendered. The judge had concluded that the Hotel Biltmont chain did not own the island that they had developed into a resort. It was determined that the church was the rightful owner based on the deeds that were placed as evidence.

The monsignor told them that the easy solution was to maintain the status quo. He put his index finger to his lips and said, "Shhhh".

At the next Rusty Kettle meeting, the question was asked,

"Father, can we be liable if we sit on the church's board and a mistake was made"?

"You're okay. The legal staff says that since you were following the terms of the court's order and you served without stipends, that you are free of any problems".

"Father, we're free of liabilities but we think the church has sinned".

"If that's the case, let's us pray for the church".

EDIE FARROW

From afar, Edie Farrow appeared to be a woman whose company one would love to have. Up close, she was distant and unfriendly. It was not because she would quickly tell you she wanted to be left alone. It was her attitude. She would not be interrupted in what she was engaged in to give anyone attention.

Edie gave strangers the brush-off almost as if she was dismissing an insect or stray animal when she told whomever stood before her –"Get! Don't bother me"! The scowl on her face was enough to have a person think that she was some sort of "ding-a-ling". In reality, that was not who she was. She was bright, well read, and purposely shielded herself from other persons. She herself lacked self-esteem. Her own insecurities told her that she was tilted towards a misanthropic nature. She didn't like people. She sometimes liked herself but not on a regular basis. Her own parents had been dirt farmers who displayed no affection for each other or for her.

Her break-away from them was accidental and proved to be rather fortunate. She was left at a gas station when she went to the restroom and discovered her parent's car gone when she returned to the gas pumps. The attendant at the gas station didn't know what to do other than to contact the police. The gas station mechanic thought that her parents would return and suggested to his boss to wait a day before calling the police. His thinking was: Why invite negative notoriety for the eleven-year-old girl?

Helped by Edie's not wanting them to call the police, the logic expressed by Craig Farrow, the mechanic, prevailed. He took the girl to his Victorian house that he owned in the back of the gas station. He introduced Edie to his wife, Camelia. Edie started to cry after she fully realized her terrible situation. The reason for her crying was not that she was left at the gas station, but that she feared that her parents would return. She was confused and did not know what was to happen to her. She just knew she didn't want the police. She didn't want to be placed in the care of other strangers.

Camelia understood Edie's feelings and explained things to her husband and to the owner of the gas station owner. It was best to allow Edie to remain with Camelia for a few hours or days. After all, they had the excuse that her parents could reappear at any time to reclaim Edie. Her parents never returned. She was enrolled at school as Edie Farrow, the last name of Craig and Camelia. The changing of her last name was to avoid detection in case there was a search for Edie.

Edie didn't like her school mates and living behind the gas station was boring in that the chores assigned to her were thought to be demeaning, i.e. sweeping, mopping, drying dishes, folding clothes, and vacuuming. Edie stayed with the Farrows for seven years. When Camelia became very sick, a sister of hers came to help Craig take care of her. The talkative sister proved to be impossible for Edie to continue living with the Farrows. She left. She was provided with several hundred dollars by Craig who told her she could return if she wished to do so. She was now almost eighteen and could pass for being older.

Edie boarded a Greyhound bus and stepped off it in Philadelphia. There she landed a job in the museum book store. The museum allowed her access to view and study their wonderful and rare collection of works of art. She self-taught herself all she could absorb about each artist and painting that was housed or exhibited there. Her other source of enjoyment took shape in appreciating and familiarizing herself with classical music. She collected hundreds of phonograph records and attended operas, movie musicals and symphony programs. All of her endeavors were attended by herself, for herself.

Years went by, and the only note-worthy changes in her life were changes in hair-dos and clothes. She remained working in lock step at the book store for eleven years. Her museum customers probably thought she was unable to speak and gracefully dismissed her robotic manner. Change would not have entered her lonely life if she had not been contacted by the Lewis and Lewis Law firm. Craig Farrow had died and left her forty-nine percent of his portion of a huge motel. It seems that years ago he had bought out the owner of the gas station and had his large lot cleared in order to construct a large motel. Since Camelia had died, Craig had willed Edie his portion of his ownership in the motel.

Edie was totally surprised because she only knew Craig as a kind man who spent his best hours under a car or under the hood of an auto. He never had clean finger nails or unspotted overalls. After Edie was advised to talk to a certain Certified Public Accountant who managed the accounts of the Thunderbird Lodge, she became more astonished. Her ownership in the property was valued at about $725,000. The Thunderbird Lodge was a profitable enterprise. Her partners were a Mr. Robert Willis, who owned 26% of the motel, and Mr. Horace Willis who owned 25%. Edie decided to go and see the property that she had inherited.

She took the Greyhound bus and it made a stop in front of the Thunderbird Lodge. It was a three-story, thirty-six units building. It was nicely landscaped and had a small outdoor pool in the back where Camelia's house used to be. When she entered the motel office, she saw a young man behind the office counter giving directions to a family on how to take the turn-off to get to Harrisburg. Edie announced herself the minute she entered.

The man behind the counter said,

"I'll be right with you. Please take a seat".

He casually talked with the family and had them fill out an evaluation form of the services rendered to them during their stay. Edie had it in mind that that guy who thought himself in charge should get a real piece of her mind.

When the family left, the man behind the counter looked Edie over and said,

"Hello, partner. I'm Robert Willis. Would you like to see the place? I can have Catrina, our head maid, show you some of the rooms. My brother, Horace, can explain the outdoor stuff. He's out there mowing the front lawn. He is also in charge of maintenance because he is handy at everything."

"You know, Robert, I used to live here before. I know the outdoors. Why don't you show me the main amenities of the motel?"

"I'd like to, but everyone is checking out at this hour, and I have to remain in the office. Check-out time is 11:00 a.m., and it is 10:41 a.m. now".

Edie went into the breakfast, laundry rooms, and looked into several suites and open rooms that the maids were readying. She went up to Horace, her other partner, and he acknowledged her and left to continue the work he was doing, and only acknowledging her by saying "I'm glad to meet you".

When she went into the office to talk with Robert, she saw a young couple registering. She saw them pay cash, pick up the room key, and head straight for the room number designated.

Edie was angry, and told Robert that those kids were going to have sex. He was letting them make us their accomplices. That was inexcusable.

"Miss Farrow, we have no right to do otherwise, and it's very acceptable to give them the key to one of our rooms. More than a third of the persons who take rooms here are gone in just a few hours. It's the way of the world. I've done the same thing many times. How about you"?

"How terrible of you to ask me such a question! I am not here to tell you about my moral code".

"Miss Farrow, why are you here? My brother and I are running the business as of now and it's profitable. You're reaping your share of dollars that we deposit at the bank".

"Mr. Willis, as a partner, I want to actively help guide our enterprise. Do you have something in mind for me to do"?

"Edie, we figure you would help with public relations. You can write brochures, newspaper and TV spots, address complaints, and instruct the maids on their responsibilities. How does that suit you? Look, Edie, you are a partner, and we'll treat you as a person in business. As a partner, we will say and act the way Horace and I have always talked and operated with each other. Please don't think we see you as a woman that requires us to change everything. We see you as a partner. Do you understand how we will relate to each other"?

"That's okay with me".

Within a period of two months, Edie began to fit into her job and, after speaking with guests, formulated a couple of ideas for adding zest and revenue to the enterprise. She told Robert that her prime idea was to convert and expand the space that housed supplies and also that the tool shed be moved to another spot so that space could be converted into a large hall. The plan that she had was to advertise to conventions, parties, weddings, on an indoor-outdoor basis. Further, Edie remarked,

"I've researched this idea and found out that no one else is offering such services".

Robert looked at her and shook his head.

"I think that's overkill. We're busy as it is. Remodeling, storing tables, tablecloths, chairs, vases, decorations, and getting a license to serve alcoholic beverages is not our cup of tea".

"Robert, I would take care of all those items. Believe me, they are not the problem you have sketched out. The profits for such an adjunct enterprise could be huge".

"The answer is NO".

"I say the answer should be YES".

"You're outvoted two to one".

Edie stomped out of the motel office and went to seek Horace. She found him spray-painting some PVC pipes at pool side.

"Horace, I presented this idea to Robert and he didn't care for it. I want to get your input".

Horace listened and told her that it was a great idea. He also indicated that he would have to have a very good reason to go against his brother. He suggested that it would be better if all three could agree on what needed to be done.

"Is that it, Horace? Am I always to be out-voted"?

"Edie, since you are talking to me, let me tell you that Robert sees you as a partner. I see you as a woman and a partner. If you get my meaning, I'd be delighted to be with you on a vote or anything else".

"What are you talking about? You want me to go to bed with you"?

"Yes. I assure you that it would be a wonderful love affair. Think it over. You might find out about the advantages we could have in having each other's company. Life is not to be lived as an agony. We are young. We can find the time to have some ecstasy".

A bribe, no less, is what Edie started to interpret. Slowly, other thoughts made her look at Horace. He was a handsome, strong, no-nonsense man. Her thoughts were troubled. He had referred to her as a woman and was overtly signaling her that he wanted her. Edie was flustered. She wanted to retreat to the original reason for seeking out Horace.

"Horace, you think about the way we can create excitement by implementing my idea about having festivities on our premises".

"Edie, that's what I want. I want to have more excitement. Stop and think about an on-going partnership that's more than just friendship".

She quickly went back to the room she used as an office and looked at herself in the large wall mirror. She was thirty. With time passing, in the end, she would be richer but would remain the very same and happy person, working her life without ever soaring in feelings. She was being asked to change her life. What should she do? She began to pace the floor to help her think. That guy has gall! She could bet he's been around. She was still a virgin because she hadn't wanted anyone to be close to her.

She thought, "Oh, why do I torture myself? Horace sees through me; he knows what I need more than I do myself. Is there a chance I can change and be more honest with myself? I like the guy. Damn it, I'm going to have him kiss me and then see".

Edie looked at herself again in the mirror. She smiled – a "first" in a long time- and quickly went out the door.

AWAY FROM THE ALLEY

Before the core of the inner city was cleared and replaced by tall structures which are now in place, there existed a complex of four and five narrow blocks that ran between regular city streets. These smelly alleys had some back entrances of companies which fronted on business streets. Also, in these alleys housing existed that was as if built in third world countries. These alleys also attracted newly arrived immigrants. Low rents were their only possible attraction. Tenants gathered in these inner city enclaves because people were from their own European countries areas and their own language was already in place there.

The new immigrants were not happy campers. They took heart in that they were in America with people like themselves. They only found work at the lower rungs of the economic ladder. They endured the fear of the bums and drunks who frequented these less traveled alleys because of the negative influences that they could have on their innocent children. These captured residents waited the work opportunities that could allow them to escape from there to the outer city.

Since parks and playgrounds were distant, kids played on narrow alley streets. Most bums and drunks knew to distance themselves from the youngsters because their solidly built fathers were as fierce as the Irish policeman who were sometimes summoned to remove them by putting them into paddy wagons. Many a drunk had to be taken to the hospital because of being caught peeing behind the garbage bins of companies. Life for these residents in this part of the city was a challenge. They didn't want to live there any longer than they had to.

The less English a person spoke and understood, the fewer his job opportunities. When a household had no bread winners, the neighbors who worked had out-of-work residents temporarily imposing on them. In some cases that was the way it was before their arrival in the USA. Tradition and faith for a better life bonded them to each other. As terrible as poverty was and is, it strengthens one's resiliency, courage, faith, and determination. Those who survived not breaking down to becoming lazy, fat and maladjusted, in time became outstanding additions to society. Some beautiful and wonderful persons had their start in the alleys that were the first stepping stones to begin new lives in America.

When Steve Plassas was born, his newly arrived parents, who rented an alley dwelling, rejoiced for their good fortune. Prior to his birth, luck had not made its appearance. Stevie was deemed the blessed sign that told his parents that renewal and better changes were on the way. Steve's father was a bricklayer and skilled at any work which required cement.

In the early years of President Roosevelt's administration, private and federal construction became wider spread. Nick Plassas happily worked his twelve-hour days. The Plassas family saved to qualify and rent a house away from their alley and moved near the school that their son would be attending later. Education was seen as the ingredient that would allow their son to reach higher rungs on the economic ladder.

Steady work for Nick allowed the Plassas family to climb out from poverty. His dad bought a 1934 Ford. The auto gave them pride when they drove around the city and to visit their former neighbors. With the freedom that they now had by owning a car, they went to the parks to picnic on Sundays. The years went by as Nick Plassas learned to drive a cement truck equipped to pull a generator.

Steve went to his elementary school where he found himself in the same grade as Athena Theodakis, his former neighbor and a family friend. Athena was the most beautiful girl that Steve had ever seen. She was the smartest girl in his class and she could jump rope for hours. She taught him how to play Hop-Scotch, and he taught her how to play Dodge-ball and Kick the Can. They were good friends and their parents visited each other to picnic in the park. Many a time while playing together, Steve saw Athena's underpants and thought of the day he could see more of her. He definitely had a crush on her.

When Athena's family moved away from their make shift alley house, the destruction ball was two weeks away from battering it into rubble. The Theodakis' family located fifteen blocks from the high school. Steve's distance to the high school was twice as far. Walking everywhere was the accepted mode of transportation for kids since the street cars that made a stop near the high school always required waiting and having to ride the bumper because other students who came a greater distance were already crowded in the street car.

At the high school, Steve played for his school's baseball team and Athena was usually there to be walked home after Steve's practice or game. They held hands and love was surely shining up their eyes. They refrained from kissing and focused on telling each other their secrets, thoughts about school, family and of the hopes they wanted to realize in the future.

In their junior year, Athena moved again. This time to a city four hundred miles away. Her father and mother went into the restaurant business. Athena, herself had to help out after school and on weekend days. The distance in miles resulted in a fade-away of their friendship. They lost complete touch with each other when Steve went to college and dated other girls. Athena hosted restaurant customers and became indispensable doing the bookkeeping and ordering for the Theodakis enterprise. Mom and Pop were in the kitchen and Athena and three waiters responded to the requests of customers. The restaurant made a good deal of money in that the Mediterranean cuisine that was served there was communicated on a customer to customer basis and resulted in attracting crowds of people to the restaurant.

Steve received his college diploma along with his teacher's credential. He applied to teach in his hometown and was accepted to teach physical education and science at the high school. His parents went to visit relatives in Greece and decided they could live very well there on the pension money they received monthly from a major construction company. They decided to reside in Greece permanently, but kept in close touch with their American born son.

Steve was in a place in life that while he enjoyed teaching, playing tennis with his friend, the principal, of his high school, he lacked that something to comfort his unrequited want. On a Friday evening when he picked up his mail, he noted a very elaborately decorated envelope amongst his bills. He feared that he knew what it contained. He opened it and saw that it was an engagement announcement from the Theodakis. Athena Artemis Theodakis was getting engaged to marry some guy whose name he didn't like: Godfrey Lloyd Goody! The engagement announcement also had a personal note from Athena:

"Hope you'll come to see my family and me. Here is my card in case you can ever break away from your commitments. We continuously think of you".

Steve uncorked a bottle of red wine and started to pour some into a glass when his arm numbed. He forgot drinking his wine. Instead, he went to the telephone to tell his principal that he had a family emergency and had to drive to Southern California and to tell them that he might miss a few days in the coming week. He packed some clothes, including his best suit, shirt and tie. He jumped into his '57 Ford Thunderbird and was off to see Athena.

In six hours, he was in front of the Theodakis' Mediterranean Restaurant. He went in and couldn't recognize any of the workers in either the main dining room or kitchen. He asked the hostess for Athena, and she looked him over and called her on the telephone.

"Athena, there is a Steve Plassas who insists on speaking with you".

The hostess hung up the phone and said that Athena was on her way and would he please wait at the bar. In five minutes, Athena was running into her restaurant. She ran directly to Steve and gave him a strong hug.

"Athena, you're not going to marry that Goody guy. I'm in love with you, and have always been in love with you. I want to marry you".

Then he kissed her hard and long and all the on-lookers decided to clap.

"Are you proposing to me"?

"Yes!"

Both left the restaurant and Athena directed him to where her car was parked. She said,

"I want to get my car back to our apartment. Please follow me".

"Wait, I want to marry you today. I want us to go to Las Vegas. Come now, no telephone calls. This time is just for the two of us."

"Steve, one of the waitresses told me about a place in Las Vegas that she recommends. I do have to make a few calls. I have to get that address and the name of the hotel that has those sexy mirror ceilings, a hot tub in the room and all that".

"Sounds great – but don't call Goody until after we are married".

"I promise".

Athena had a sizeable suitcase and the necessary addresses that her waitress friend had told her. They drove all night to Las Vegas and by morning, they were at the Chapel of the Rainbow Sky. They actually had to wake up the minister and his wife. The minister directed them to the courthouse to sign necessary papers. He needed them to return after 11:00 a.m.

When they returned to the chapel and asked for a room in order to change their clothes. After more papers were signed, everything was ready. The minister asked what kind of wedding they had decided upon. They looked at each other and said,

"Sir, just get on with it".

"Do you have a ring"? the minister's wife asked.

Steve was about to say, "no" when he heard a loud voice from one of the witnesses. The familiar voice was from his father who trumped "yes"! He displayed the ring to his son.

"How is this possible? How is it that you are here and have the ring? Dad, I thought you and Mom were still in Greece!"

"No, we have been guests of the Theodakis' for a week. Mama Theodakis was hugging her daughter and her Dad was waiting his turn. Steve looked around and said,

"I don't get it!"

All the family witnesses smiled and then laughed. Athena covered her face with her hands and said,

"Steve, you know that anything is fair in love and war. I had to think how to get you here. You were always the one. Our parents knew it, and I know it. We just needed you to get into step with us. We concocted the plot to move you into the action we all wanted you to take. We're all here in Las Vegas because we all agreed that you would not allow me to marry a guy named Godfrey Lloyd Goody. You and I were bonded from the days of our living in that terrible alley. You know, Steve, there was only one engagement announcement made to be mailed. It was to you. There is no such person as Goody. We made him up".

Steve said,

"I guess you all know me well. I guess my feelings haven't been a secret to anyone.

I've been thankfully outsmarted. Baby, you guys just hit a home run"!

A TRIP TOO FAR

Persons who knew or met Milo Valenti for the first time responded gleefully to his good looks and friendliness. He seemed so alert, glad, and comfortable to be in the company of persons of all ages. His eyes and face danced when he laughed, and his charismatic manner pulled those around him into an embracing spell.

His father saw Milo sprout and form his numerous attributes during his twelve years. At his young age, he certainly could converse about the music and classic literature that Tony, his father, had him listen and discuss. Each of them was motivated to learn as much about thoughts and moods which were handed to them by the many notable literary geniuses who contributed masterpieces as legacies for the pleasure of everyone.

Milo's mother died when he was a few months short of being three years old. Milo thought he could recall her fragrance and her wonderful voice when she sang to him in her soft notes. However, it was his father who extended himself to informally educate him and helped him fully develop his potential.

A friend of the Valentis, who by profession was an astronomer, invited Tony and Milo to dinner at his home in a neighboring town. At that dinner, Dr. Asfelt indicated that he was going to his proclaimed geographical paradise to fish in the largest California lake for Eagle Lake trout. He described the catches he had made in earlier years and how his mouth watered at the thought of biting into the native trout's red meat. The professor noticed that Milo was sitting on the edge of his chair during his description of his impending field trip to the lake. Milo asked his Dad if, at some point, they could journey to Eagle Lake. The professor was delighted to hear this wish from Milo and added that if they wanted to go, he had all the necessary camping equipment to share with them. They only needed to transport some of the camping supplies and obtain their fishing licenses.

After loading a large tent, sleeping bags, mattresses, a folding table and chairs, the professor's travel arrangements were to precede them by a day. The professor took the cooler, food supplies, fishing rods, and lures and would ready their camp. The day Tony and Milo took the long trip, their Volkswagen bus slowly navigated the highway to transgress the mountain summit. Milo and Tony were happily engaged in telling riddles to each other.

They also commented their awe of the garden that nature had produced. The greenery had a hundred shades of that one color. The landscape was embellished with more interest by having splashes of wild yellow and blue flowers sporadically placed in the spaces between the trees.

Instantly, their happiness was curtailed. A motorcyclist landed on their windshield with such force that Milo was propelled from the vehicle onto the metal rail which bordered the highway. The motorcyclist continued his flight over the embankment and most likely made his last ride. Tony was bleeding but able to open his bus door and run to his son's side. Milo was near-dead, but alive. His body was broken, and he had a deep cut on the back of his head.

In minutes, the Highway Patrol was on the scene calling for additional resources. In a short time, a helicopter arrived and took Milo to a Bay Area hospital. Tony was transported by ambulance to another hospital, and then to the hospital where Milo was being attended. Milo had been operated on his legs, and his deep head wound was closed with stitches and staples. He was unconscious and connected to several machines.

Tony could not go home. He had to remain next to Milo. He was devastated. He never left Milo's side. Tony could only cry and pray. He had hope for Milo to recover because the doctors and nurses frequently looked in on their unconscious patient. The hospital staff was very caring and took time to insure Milo's comfort.

Milo's still body gave no sign that he was in a contest with the Dark Shadow that appeared to transport him away from his hospital bed. The Dark Shadow told Milo that the end of his journey on earth was over. His other journey would begin in a matter of minutes. Milo was powerless to move any part of his body to show his father that he was unwilling to leave him without a quick and loving goodbye.

The Dark Shadow read Milo's thoughts and attempted to soften his departure by telling Milo that his father would join him in eleven days.

"How is that? He is very young, healthy and energetic".

The Dark One transmitted that Tony Valenti would commit suicide as he could not go further in life without his great kid by his side. Milo messaged his thoughts to the Dark Phantom that he needed to talk with his father. He didn't want his father to die because of his absence. The Dark One indicated that he didn't have any power that could allow him to talk to his father. According to the Dark Shadow, that was impossible. He had to leave quickly and travel away.

At the same instant, Milo was being hugged by his Dad. The Dark Shadow who must have been rather new at his vocation inappropriately messaged to Milo:

"Oh, what a shame! Your history potential indicates that if you had not been in that automobile accident, you would have become a great author of stories. You would have been a great writer and genuine man of letters. Your essays would have been revered throughout the world. Once I touch you, all that potential will disappear and perhaps will be left for others to do many years from now".

"Dark Shadow, please, please…I don't care about that now. I want to talk to my father".

"I'm sorry I can't do that".

His father was still hugging him and gently showering Milo with his own tears. Then, the fences that held Milo's voice within him collapsed.

"Dad, I love you so much. You need to hold me in our memory and be a grateful, happy person. You must stay healthy and carry me in your heart as long as you can stay alive. I'll be with you at all times. You will be unable to see me, but you will always sense my presence. I love you. Get over the fact that you can't see me. We will continue to live together. Please don't ever interrupt the love we now share. Bye".

The Dark Shadow was appalled! His delay and inappropriate messaging to Milo had interfered with what was to take place in eleven days. The Dark shadow now didn't understand if Tony's dates had been altered.

Before he got into more problems, he touched Milo, and both took hold of an invisible beam that sped them away.

THE NOSE BLEED

I have noticed that the older my Dad becomes, the more he's into exaggeration about his personal views and accomplishments. For example, on Saturday, he looks me in my eyes and related his latest praiseworthy experience. This is what he said in his own words.

About three weeks ago, I walked several big city blocks to the grocery store to buy avocados in order to have guacamole with tortilla chips with my four o'clock Martini.

As soon as I arrived at the store, I felt that I had a runny nose and came quickly to the discovery that I had a bloody nose. My bloody shirt indicated that I was bleeding profusely. I held my nose tightly in order to attempt to stop the nose bleed. I walked outside the store and found a bench. I sat there with my head down and pinching my nose. However, instead of the blood going out of my nose, it was spilling into and out of my mouth. It was then that I knew I was in real trouble.

I heard a voice ask me, "Sir, are you all right? Do you need help?"

I looked up and saw a gorgeous light skinned Afro-American lady in a designer jogging outfit. I told her that I had a nose bleed and it was giving me a problem because I took blood thinners. I needed her to call 911 for me because I did not have a cell phone. She informed me that she knew where there was a hospital. She offered to drive me there.

"I might get your car all dirty, but thank you. Can you just have the ambulance service take me to the emergency room?"

"Nonsense", she replied.

She told me to sit tight while she put her groceries away. In seconds, she was opening the door to an old but classic Mercedes automobile. She had covered the passenger seat with plastic bags from her groceries and gave me a roll of paper towels to use for my nose. In a hurried manner, she drove me to the emergency hospital in silence.

I was lucky in that the emergency hospital staff was not burdened by the usual number of hurting patients. I was escorted directly into an inner room which had nurses and a physician. I was there forty-five minutes and released with gauze nose plugs which made me appear to be a casualty in a prize fight. I expected to call a taxi to take me home. However, my savior, the gorgeous lady, waited for my dismissal and said,

"I'll take you home".

I couldn't believe such concern and kindness. "What was this about? I asked myself".

As we approached her car, she asked how I felt. I took a good look at her and thought to myself that maybe she was a movie star or an entertainer. I asked her for her name. She said her name was Yvonne Thompson.

"Yvonne, you are beautiful. I can't believe you are spending your Sunday looking after a stranger who needed assistance".

"Don't worry about me. I have nothing better to do. I am glad to be of some service to you".

As she drove into my driveway, I thanked her and told her I would normally kiss her cheek, but that kind of thanks was out of the question with my large nose plugs hanging down from my nostrils. To my surprise, she got out of her car and entered my house with me, explaining that the nurse and doctor thought I should be watched for a period of time to insure that the nose plugs had stopped the bleeding.

I offered Yvonne coffee, juice or a soft drink. She said that she would make tea for us. Yvonne moved with grace and seemed to understand where everything was in my kitchen. She made us tea and even found a package of Graham crackers to place on the kitchen table. I asked Yvonne where she lived and she told me that she now lived in Seattle, Washington. She was here to visit her mother.

"Oh", I said. "What do you do back home?"

She laughed and said, "You were right when you guessed that I was in the entertainment business. I'm a pole dancer".

"You mean, you strip naked and dance for paying customers?"

"Does that bother you?" she asked.

"I don't think so"

"You see, I make a lot of money dancing, and besides, I've never ever sold myself. I don't mind being naked because I'm well-built and do not have family except my mother. Maybe someday a big spender will want me for myself, and that is as good a plan as any, don't you think?"

"Gee, I think it's a great reason for me to take a trip to Seattle."

I was sorry I verbalized my thought because she seemed to be a serious lady.

"Look, I'll tell you what. By Thursday, you will be back to normal, at least that's what the nurse told me. I'll save you the trip money, and I'll come here and dance for you after you take me to a nice lunch".

My eyes got big for the deal I was getting. The nose bleed had its opportunistic side. We finished our tea and crackers. Afterwards, she washed the dishes. She gave me her goodbye and said she would see me at

11:30 a.m. on Thursday. Then, she left and I stood at my door watching her drive away.

Was Yvonne going to dance naked in my living room to thrill me as my imagination extrapolated? I guess I had to wait for Thursday to find out. My nose plugs came out of my nose on Tuesday, and I looked almost normal again. When Thursday came, I waited for 11:30 a.m. to see if there was noteworthy reality to this strange happening. All was not understandable, but life is in a different gear these days from what I remembered it to be during my hay days.

When 11:30 a.m. came, I was about to laugh at myself, when the classic model Mercedes drove into my driveway. I opened my front door and saw a blonde, blue-eyed woman of about 50-something get out of her car. She could have been a young Jane Fonda, or some other feminist specimen from a gymnasium or fashion magazine.

"Hi, I'm Yvonne's mother. I'm Vera Thompson". Then, she added,

"Yvonne had to go back to Seattle because a Dallas oilman was boisterously rattling the club's management because she was on the outside advertising posters and not present within."

Yvonne had told her mother about Dallas Danny, the oil engineer who loved spending his money on toys and entertainment. She also added that Danny liked her a lot. That said, I took her to the airport.

"She told me all about you and the deal she made. I'm here to take her place. Shall we go to lunch?"

I didn't know what to say or what to do. All I could do was have her drive directly to the very nice Italian restaurant where we had a great lunch. Vera was a loquacious woman. She was carefree and had traveled. She was casual to the point that it seemed that I had known her for a lengthy period of time. She was also very good looking. While not the beauty of her offspring, she was a shapely muscular wonder.

Once the bill was paid, she said,

"O.K., let's go to your home and let me entertain you."

That's when I got cold feet and kissed her on the cheek and thanked her for being such a good sport. Vera thanked me and pinched my cheek and said,

"I'll confess that I never learned to dance. Going to your home probably would have been disastrous".

She left telling me to have a good life.

"Vera, please give my regards to Yvonne when you see her".

Maybe...... I was probably saved from having another nose bleed and the entire situation with the Thompsons proved to be better than any other fancies I could concoct.

As I said at the beginning, I don't know whether to believe my Dad or not. I wish I was as lucky as he or have the kind of thoughts which entertain him.

I think I'll call Seattle and check out whether there is an entertainer such as my Dad described to me.

THE PATH BETWEEN

The Hicks homestead sat on a grassy plain carved by one of the tributaries of the Bitterroot River. The small lake formed when higher terrain blocked the runoff from the river. That location seemed to be the perfect place to build their cabin. The Hicks: Jacob, Justina, and Jacob's brother Andrew, had settled there nearly eighteen years ago. Josh had been born sixteen years ago. Andrew died of pneumonia four years ago. Since they settled there, none of them had ventured from the mountains that walled them in to live in their rustic dwellings.

Originally, Jacob and Justina and Jacob's brother had journeyed thousands of miles from far-off Kentucky. The three Hicks traveled driving their three saddle and seven pack horses in search of a homestead. Over the years, pain was taken to maintain watchful care of their essential horses. However, their precious animals were skillfully killed by the sneak attacks of bears and cougars.

Jacob had learned to set traps for deer and small forest animals. This important skill was taught to Josh by his father. Josh grew up a woodsman who knew how to survive by fishing, making and setting traps, and identifying edibles provided by the grasses and special trees located at the escarpment of the mountain range.

Justine was from a small town and, as soon as their homestead was established, seemed to take root on the spot on which life was to be lived.

She took ownership of most domestic tasks and extended herself to assist Jacob in his pursuits.

Josh worked individually from his parents. He was not a builder of cabins, sheds, or mud rooms. He knew the forest, its plants, and where to set traps for deer, raccoons, hares, squirrels, badgers, and opossums.

Justina's workaholic ways were attributed to being strong in body. When in motion, she thought only of completing tasks. She was not formally educated, but was pragmatic and not inclined to be emotional about anything. She washed, cleaned, made clothes from hides, skinned animals, and smoked their meat. She also took her end of the crosscut and bucksaw to assist in the cutting of logs. She also made adobe to cover the holes between the logs and walls of their cabin. She tied the logs together with leather straps to make a raft and also bind rough household furniture.

Jacob was the problem solver. He improvised how to make the chimney, heat the house, build extensions to the cabin, and helped catch frogs, make soap and lye, preserve fur and hides, plane logs, and pen the trapped forest animals in order to eat them when they regained their health.

Josh had no way of obtaining a formal education. He was not aware that he was deprived by not being able to hear or visualize the history of his parents' backgrounds. He lacked necessary mental triggers that family normally provides. The result of not hearing stories or commentaries of life put him at a verbal disadvantage. His parents' speaking and writing skills were limited to what they knew. An "x" was used by his Dad and that was also his way of thinking about writing his name. Like his father, Josh was a problem solver. His forest traps were hand crafted and well planned. He usually put his "x" on a nearby tree in order to express to the Indian families, who were their neighbors, that he set his animal traps nearby.

Most of the time, Josh would be on his own. He loved the fact that he knew how to walk the wilderness and make do with his trappings and water from several small waterholes that he frequented on his overnighters.

On a crisp November day, Josh was about four miles in the mountain foothills when suddenly a rapid change in the weather took place. It began to snow hard. Josh needed to find some kind of cover. The forest was not a safe place in a blizzard and, therefore, when the murder-some elements were in an uproar, he headed towards the mountains. Josh had to seek higher ground to search for rock overhangs or crevices in order to outwit the challenging storm.

He was in luck as he discovered and entered an opening in the mountain. Crawling into that wide hole, he entered a sizeable large cave where he could stand up. The cave had a very bad smell. There were hundreds of bats hanging from the ceiling, and the cave floor was carpeted with their droppings. Once he consumed his packed provisions, he had to rely on clubbing bats off of the cave's ceiling, so he could cook them for his nourishment. The parts of the bats that he discarded were used to fuel his fire.

The storm lasted six full days. The ground on the outside of the cave was heavy with ice and snow. Josh decided to remain in the cave an additional three days because his leather leggings were not sufficiently high on his legs to keep his feet dry.

On the fourth day, he chanced leaving his shelter. He could smell himself in the fresh air and could not stand his own odor. He wanted to have a change in his diet. The glaring whiteness of the terrain caused him some directional confusion for returning to his cabin. He looked for his mark on the trees. Instead of finding his markings on the trees, he found he was in a part of the wilderness that had traps set by his Shoshone neighbors. While Josh realized that he was about ten miles off-course from his cabin, he corrected himself and turned to walk in the direction he now knew that he should take.

A noise he heard was made by Feathered Arrow, a Shoshone who was the leader of the small clan of Indians that resided eight miles from his homestead. Feathered Arrow knew Josh was away from his land. In the past, he had seen Josh many times in the forest. He motioned Josh to follow him. Both of them entered the Indian camp, and all the Indians (about thirteen) gathered around to hear an explanation of why Josh was there. Through mimicry, Josh attempted to explain himself. Everyone laughed at his pantomime. The small group of Indians was composed of four middle-age men and nine women. Three of the women seemed to be teenagers. Josh was grabbed by three Indian women, and his clothes were removed to further laughter. His clothes needed to be washed. He was scrubbed with deer skin chamois. He was then wrapped in Indian garb and invited to eat venison stew.

After their meal, Feathered Arrow introduced him around. Josh was a hit with the Indian damsels. He particularly liked the looks of one of the teen-age girls. It was his thought that she was the rarest of girls. In fact, he had never seen others of her gender outside of his mother. That teen-age girl's big eyes were looking straight at him. Feathered Arrow took him over to meet her. Then he gave her his smelly clothes to clean.

After hours of smoking from a pipe in the company of men, he was shown to one of the log frame shelters which had stretched animal skins between sturdy tree poles. Inside the floor covered with skins were piles of hides. Josh figured it was where he was supposed to sleep. He laid down under the hides and was about to go to sleep when he heard the voice of Feathered Arrow speaking to someone outside the shelter. A person entered his sleeping quarters and put his own clean clothes at his side. Josh had seen his father pull his mother into bed, and he figured that he could do the same to the girl who he knew he liked.

At the coming of dawn, Josh was able to study his young Indian girl who had kept him warm all night. She also had helped him remove his clothes to insure her own warmth. The other ladies who were at nearby shelters stayed awake all night because Big Deer Eyes made audible pleasure-cries that they could hear.

In the morning, the girl made Josh stand up to put on the same clean clothes that he had on when he entered her camp. Feathered Arrow gave him a hand when he came out of the shelter. The same stew meat of the evening before was served. When Josh was ready to leave, Big Deer Eyes was at his side. Feathered Arrow and two other older females were also ready to accompany Josh on his walk to his cabin. Everyone carried bundles and hides except for Feathered Arrow and Josh.

When Josh and his party of Indian friends arrived at his homestead, Jacob greeted his guests and was not surprised to see that Josh had returned from some sort of ordeal in the wilderness. Justina hugged Josh without fanfare and retained her emotions to herself. Justina *did* look hard at the young Indian who was about fifteen or sixteen years of age and assumed that Josh had been in her company during the time he was gone. Jacob knew differently. He saw what Feathered Arrow placed on the ground. He laid out many hides, smoked meats and two spears. His treasures included a pipe and some clothes for Big Deer Eyes. He was happy. Jacob turned to Josh and said,

"Did you know you have married this girl?"

Josh was bewildered. Jacob brought him to his senses by telling him that he better comply with the marriage arrangement if he wished to continue to live in peace with the neighboring Indians. Feathered Arrow and his ladies departed, leaving Big Deer Eyes with the Hicks.

Big Deer Eyes was a cheerful person. She had straight black hair that fell to her waist when untied. She had a prominent nose and wide cheeks, and her eyes were big and beautiful. The next night was spent as it was when he unknowingly lost his bachelorhood. In the morning, Josh went into the forest to review his traps. Big Deer Eyes was afraid of Justina so she ran to be in the forest with Josh. Three of the forest traps had caught two raccoons and a skunk which they discarded.

On their return to the cabin, Justina took Big Deer Eyes by the hand and gave her clothes to wash in the lake. Justina looked into her daughter-in-law's eyes and said,

"You have to be a Christian now, so your new name is Jeari; you are Jeari".

Justine lifted her finger towards Big Deer Eyes and pointed to her and said, "Jeari, you Jeari".

The way to the Shoshone camp became a well-travelled path. Josh and Jeari were frequent visitors there because Jeari wanted to be taught how to soften deer skins. Josh was interested to learn how to shoot arrows with a bow, and how to make spear and arrow heads. A year went by and contact between the Hicks and the Shoshones halted only when the cold and heavy snow of winter limited the activities which could take place.

One day, late in the spring when Jacob and Justina were cutting wood to re-supply the woodshed, Jacob looked at the big black birds circling in the sky. He immediately called everyone together. He had to dress in his heavy winter clothes, clean the oil off his rifle to go to Feathered Arrow's camp. His cartridges were almost all gone but sufficient for his needs to deal with any possible problem. He told Josh and the women that they must stay close to the cabin. Josh was instructed to keep his bow, spear, knife with him at all times. Josh wanted to go with his father, but was told he had to remain to take care of his mother and pregnant wife. Jacob also stated that he might be away for several days.

Five days went by before Jacob returned home with a young Indian girl and two additional rifles and several boxes of ammunition. The girl carried two pairs of manufactured shoes and her own clothes in a back pack. The girl seemed to be traumatized. When the full story was told in bits and pieces, this is what was said to have happened.

The girl and another woman had been raped by two white pioneers. The trappers were both killed by Jacob because they had murdered all of the other Indians. They were in the process of stealing all of the best skins and hides and some food provisions when they were surprised by Jacob, who had observed them for about an hour before he took his action. The bodies of the Indians had been dragged to a ravine, and the buzzards were dealing with them. The older Indian lady who had been abused ran to the ravine and killed herself. She stabbed herself through the heart and died next to her husband.

At first the young girl was hysterical but was loudly ordered to help Jacob pile dry wood and place the slain Indian bodies on the enormous stack of firewood. The wood was set on fire and Feathered Arrow and his followers turned into ashes.

At the onset, the lone Shoshone survivor was not welcomed. However, Jacob figured where she could sleep and have Jeari begin to teach her the hundreds of nouns she now knew in the language of the Hicks. When Justina delivered Jeari's baby boy, the new baby Hicks was named Jeremiah. The rescued Indian girl now had to be called "Josefa" and helped make clothes and a sleeping basket for Jeremiah. She was basically a nanny so that Jeari could maintain most of her outdoor duties.

Conversation was never a big part of their lives. Harmony and respect were far more in evidence.

Jeremiah changed Justina into a happier lady and watchful grandmother. Jacob was now the father of four and full of some ambitious undertakings.

Josh and Jeari's caring for one another grew with the presence and bonding that Jeremiah taught them.

Love was in their lives, and they were a real family.

FOLLOWING THE LINES
ON THE FLOOR

I went to Dr. Point's office for the fifth time about my same persistent problem. He was an internist, but I could tell that my problem was stomping him. My medical problem was that my severe and massive effluviums were abnormal and erratic, so much so that the public was in jeopardy when I ventured from the house.

Dr. Storey Point said,

"We tried all of the standard remedies that usually correct your condition. You might try Dr. Harvey since he is a renowned Gastro-Intestinal Specialist. and he is part of our group. He has achieved miracles in this area of his specialization. I would have recommended him previously, but he's a Catholic Irish, Irish. By that I mean he is old country. It's been reported to me that while he may have some sort of Irish phantoms, he continues to be a top-notch Gastro-Intestinal Specialist."

"Doctor, if he help me find a way to get far from the pot, I'll sing 'Danny Boy' to him".

After filing out half of ream of papers about who insured me and listing the pharmaceutical products I ingested, I received the okay to see Dr. Harvey. Dr. Harvey's receptionist opened his office door for me, and Dr. Harvey was at the entrance. He shook my hand. He said in his charismatic Irish brogue,

"Follow the white lines on the floor to the chair you are to sit in".

I looked at the white lines that went away from the chair before they formed a straight line to the chair he wanted me to sit in. I had already been appraised that Dr. Harvey was a very good doctor. He was an Ireland-born Irish, Irish, and I wanted to do whatever he said I needed to do. I adhered to his elaborate lines to get to a chair that was only about fifteen feet from the entrance to his office. Dr. Harvey, himself, followed yellow lines to sit behind his small desk.

I told him my problem and he indicated that my problem was ordinary for an "old fart of seventy-five". However, he had a remedy, and if in a month I was not cured, he would take another approach in order for me to again be in control of the bacteria that were inflating me. I thanked him, and he asked me to go to another room to take a three-hour breath test. I would just have to put my lips together and blow into a tube every twenty minutes. A week after that test, he called me and told me that I had killed all my good bacteria and the ghoulish bacteria from down under were now in charge of my body.

"Doctor, what do I do? I have to be free to walk in the world without adding propulsion and noise making".

"Are you Roman Catholic" he asked?

"No, but if you require it, I'll be Catholic", I responded.

"Too bad", he said. "I just wanted to relate the fact that Juan Diego's faith in the Virgin Mary of Guadalupe sustained him to be free of problems. Manuel, Mexicans' faith and thinking help cure what ails him. Do you remember the story of the Virgin making her appearance to Juan Diego? Remember that"?

"I heard that story but didn't give it any significance when I heard it".

"Manuel, you don't have to be Roman Catholic to know that faith heals."

I let it go, but I didn't understand what he meant.

This unconventional doctor gave me a special diet to follow and asked me to report back to him in four weeks. The diet did its work minimally. In three weeks, I was tired of being a menace to the nice persons at my company.

When I kept my next appointment to see Dr. Harvey, I noticed that the line to my chair was more intricate from the last time I was at his office. I had to go around the office several times before I could sit down on that chair that was only a few feet from his door. I saw that the doctor himself moved himself in a most round-about way to his desk. Now that I had seen Dr. Harvey three times, I asked him

'Why do the lines on the floor keep changing"?

He said,

"I'm moving to a much larger office next month, and you wouldn't have to take such circuitous routes that we have to use now. Remember that I asked you if you believed the story of Juan Diego? The reason that the Virgin of Guadalupe appeared to Juan Diego is because he believed in her. Manuel, the environment in which we are raised largely determines how and what we embody within ourselves. I just wanted you to know that if you believe in our cultural ways (and what we inherit because of where we are born and who we are born to) governs the way we are enhanced as persons. Well, I'm a believer that knowledge comes to us in many ways and directions. You know that what you tell me is confidential. However, the advantage is yours because you don't have to treat the content of our office visits as being sacred".

"Dr. Harvey, I'm here for you to do whatever you prescribe. I don't tell my friends that I'm here or that I'm being treated for these unwholesome problems".

"OK, I came from Ireland and I had the good fortune that my Puka came with me. There was no problem until he met a Welsh Puka and now my office is filled with their offspring. What's why I'm moving to a larger office. Manuel, do you comprende? My lines are compromised, as the Puka families grow in numbers. They have agreed not to interfere with me if I take care in having them stepped upon by my patients. Every time more Puka babies arrive, I have to modify the lines on the floor".

"Doctor, did these Puka go to the University of California when you studied there"?

"No, my Puka was single then and stayed in my apartment reading all my medical books. However, I also discussed the crux of learning with him which I came away with from class lectures or laboratory work.

Now, for our next step that we need to undertake. We need to narrow the passage between your small and large intestines. This can be done with laser surgery. There is no worry about being in any kind of jeopardy. Please be at this hospital in the surgical center at 6:00 a.m. next Tuesday".

I kept the appointment. Dr. Harvey was already in his surgical gear, his hair covered and he was wearing a cloth meshed mask on his face. He told me I would not need anesthesia. I saw Dr. Harvey leave from behind the elaborate machine. He later came back and said, "All done".

"Doctor, I didn't feel anything. This is a great scientific innovation".

He winked at me and said to me,

"There is no one better at using this equipment than my Puka".

"Dr. Harvey, how do I thank your Puka."

"Give him a smile and two thumbs up. If happy days return to you, you may want to send me a bushel of carrots".

IN SEARCH OF FRIENDSHIP

Irma was in one of her frequent funks. It was difficult to snap out of depression when her thinking kept boomeranging to the mess her life was in. Common sense could have aided her if she didn't give into her anxieties. The way she tried to cope with her pain of inadequacies was to allow her thoughts to vaporize by smoking weed.

It was difficult for Irma to work her four days at the hair salon. She usually worked Wednesday through Saturday. Irma was good at dealing with older ladies who had used her services for years. She, herself, had been in the business for over twenty years. The last eleven years, she worked for Morris who owned the hair salon and had a good reputation for cutting and styling the hair of younger women.

Morris was openly gay and loved to gossip with his clientele. Because Morris loved to gossip, Irma held back telling him of her loneliness. Irma recognized that Morris had to be himself and didn't fault him in any way. Morris was a very nice person and had always treated her with respect. Once in a while, Morris had to call her to tell her he wouldn't be able to come to work. At such times, Irma had to do what she could to accommodate his appointments. Irma was a good team player. When at work, her fast pace didn't allow her to look inward to mentally extract her short comings.

However, when Sunday and Monday came around, personal time reverted to self-assessing her life. She compulsively worried going forward in an unpredictable life and the annoyance she had that her body was beginning to age. It was when alone that she became depressed. She hated to look into the mirror and admit that her youthful looks were gone. When her thoughts caused her pain, she inhaled the magic dragon to give flight to her boring outlook.

On Monday, her telephone rang. The ringing was hurtful to her aching head. She answered the telephone hoping that Morris was not going to ask her to work Tuesday for him.

"Irma, this is Tommy Wyle, Morris' friend. I'm calling you because Morri is in the hospital. We were in a car wreck, and he got the worst of it. He broke an ankle, several ribs, and is in a neck brace. I'm okay. I just have some cuts on the top of my head. Morris wants you to know that you can help him by taking over the salon until he gets the okay to be released from the hospital".

"Oh my gawd! What hospital is he in"?

"He's at Kaiser".

Irma drank several cups of black coffee, dressed, and headed out the door on the way to the hospital. Irma went straight to Morris' room. Another man was there. He told Irma that he was Tommy. She could tell that Tommy had been crying. Morris was asleep. Tommy described the accident to Irma. He had been driving and saw the bicyclist just in time to swerve to avoid hitting the bike. As he swerved, his car took a spin and ended up on the opposite side of the road in front of incoming autos. One car hit the side of the car where Morris sat. Another car took off the back bumper of our vehicle. It was my fault.

"I'm so sorry, Irma. Do you think this hospital has a cafeteria? I need to get something in my stomach".

A cleaning lady overheard Tommy and told them where the cafeteria was located.

Tommy paid for their two breakfasts. Irma could tell that he was still shaken because his hand trembled and he hardly was able to use the fork to pick up his scrambled eggs. He looked at Irma and said,

"I have to be a work at 11:30 a.m. I don't feel like it. Maybe you can help me look after Morri"

"Tommy, what kind of work do you do"?

"I own my own shop. I'm an antiquarian. I own that big store at Market and Third – "Finders, Keepers".

"Look, Tommy, after Morris wakes up, I can help you since the salon is closed today. Since I do not know anything about rare books, I'll just do what you direct me to do".

"That would be nice, since I have a couple of orders coming in and have to wrap up one book that I have to send out by mail".

Morris did wake up. Tommy held his hand and told him how sorry he was. Irma took in how good a friend Tommy was. He was a genuine person. Tommy and Irma drove their respective cars to Irma's apartment because parking was impossible where Finders-Keepers was located. They then walked to a bus stop and took the bus downtown. Tommy's body had aches and pains, and he appreciated the way Irma followed directions. He noted that she treated each book carefully. There were hardly any customers. They had time to sit and talk. Irma took a chance and asked,

"Tommy, do you and Morris gossip a lot"?

"Morri does tell about his lady customers. It works out because I am a good listener. I'm not an interesting person. I don't talk much. I'm used to reading. I'm afraid to talk about other people. It is my thought that if I talk about them, they will talk about me. I'd rather not talk about others because it is not of interest to me. I'd rather be like wallpaper and stick to what is to be found in archives".

"Tommy, I need a friend. I need a friend that will listen to my thoughts. Can you do that for me? I'd rather Morris not know what I will express to you and you allow me to let my hair down".

"Irma, I'd be proud to be your friend. You must know that I may not be very good at talking. I have never talked to any woman because they have steered away from me. I guess they see something in my mannerisms that they don't trust. I must tell you that I, too, can admit that I don't always make good judgments".

"Tommy, how old do you think I am"?

"I am terrible at guessing people's age. I do better knowing the age of books. I would guess you're younger than forty".

"You are correct. I'm thirty-nine. I've never been married. I'm at a desperate age. I don't know how to make friends. The people who come to the salon are all in relationships. I don't know how to continue to be by myself. I get disgusted with myself because I know that as time moves along, I'll get more uninteresting in my appearance. I want a man. I don't know if I should change my behavior and start going to church, to bars, and to dance halls. I don't know if I should dress to show off my best part of me – my legs and my cleavage. I need everything that's inside me to come out. I want to share my feelings with a significant other. But where is he"?

"Irma, I'm not the one who knows anything. I'm very ignorant about explaining the way to adjust to life. I'm a complete dodo. I've only been with Morri. He's is the guy who has ideas and takes me everywhere. I'd be in a rut if it were not for him. Irma, I'll do anything to help you. But I've never read a book that explains modern un-neighborly behavior. The pace of the world outside of my shop and home is so different. I, too, am afraid to be without Morris. Without him, I would be done".

"Tommy, I understand. I need you to listen and do your best to understand the words that I use. Do you understand depression"?

"Only a little. I look forward to when the store closes and I can go home and listen to Morri entertain me by telling about the behaviors he hears about at the salon. It's just Morri and me, his stories, my books".

"Tommy, depression is the toughest, deepest state of being. To me, it's like having to deal with my own personal garbage. I don't like to look at myself because of the narrowness in my life's orbit. At my age, I should have had several proposals to marry. I've had a legitimate one. Men see me as maidenly, or too dark, or too light to meet their personal biases. Tommy, I tell you that I'm at a desperate point in life and, if things don't change, I will slip into the sagging age with less hope to encounter happiness. This is what I see at the salon. Ladies with double chins, wrinkled arms, graying hair, and wearing jeans to cover their fatty legs and back sides. I don't want to go there. I want out of being lonely. I don't want to be talking about a dog or a cat as if they are part of family. I want someone who cares for me as I am".

"Irma, some persons who come into the store want to have a rare book only because the copies that exist are numbered. They think that by having a first edition of a rare book, they will have what they can say no one else has what they have. To such persons, that somehow makes everything okay in their unbalanced world. Of course, I am not speaking of genuine collectors who walk a different path to find beauty in the form of books written with effort and purpose. Irma, you know how Morri talks about people. I know what he told me about you. Would it be terrible of me if I told you that he believe you are a super worker? He really likes you as a peer. He understands your worth as a person. Next to me, he likes you best. You know that he can't love you. I'm that lucky person".

"Thank you for telling me that Morri is a friend. I like him, too. I don't know if I can be as good as he is with all the young ladies that only want him to do their hair. He really is good at what he does. He's a very nice guy and you are lucky to share a life with him. You're both great because you know about each other and yourselves. Tommy, maybe after Morris returns to work, I can visit you here at your store. If I find that you're busy I wouldn't take up your time. If you have the time, I'll just say "hello" and visit you instead of having a reefer. Opening up to you has not been difficult. You are a good listener. Of course, I respect that you are not able to give me advice. I understand your explanation for not being able to do more than just being an interested listener".

The shop door opened, and it was Mr. Connley.

"Hi, Tommy, did my book come in"?

"Oh, yes. It's been here for a week"

Tommy asked Irma to get it from a drawer under the counter. Irma gently put the book on the counter. Mr. Connley was overjoyed when he examined the condition of the book he ordered. He made out a check for a very large amount. He took his bagged book and quickly left.

"What was that Robinson Crusoe book about"?

"Oh, Irma, It was a first edition of Robinson Crusoe. It's about a sole survivor of a ship wreck who made it to a remote, uninhabited island. Later, he saved a cannibal from a terrible death. He made friends with the cannibal because he was his company. They made the most of their togetherness".

"How interesting. Maybe not being too choosey is part of what not to be at thirty-nine".

"Irma, as of yesterday, I only knew your name. Please think of me as a friend. You can visit me anytime. I'll keep our friendship separate so that you have no reason to think I'll share our thoughts with Morri".

"Tommy, you have helped me immensely by listening to me. You have my secrets. For that, you deserve a hug and a kiss."

Irma kissed Tommy on the cheek. He looked at her and said,

"Not since my mom kissed me has any lady kissed this bearded face. Irma, let me give you this".

"What is it"?

"It is a charm that supposedly has magnetic properties that brings people together. I never used it from fear it would complicate my relationship with Morri. It's yours now because I think it might bring you luck. It's very old and belonged to happy people who lived on the island of Okinawa.

"That's exactly what I want. I have to go to the salon and vacuum the floor before tomorrow when the first batch of women arrive. Remember, I'm off on Mondays and Tuesdays, and I can visit you or help you when you need an extra hand.

Tommy, I feel so much better than when I left home this morning. Thanks for being my friend".

CAROL'S CARROT CAKE

I'm the kind of person that when I hear a melodious song for the first time, I pay good attention. Then, swirling in my head it gets repeated time and time again. I involuntarily find myself humming the adhesive melody without being conscious of my fixation. In addition to this idiosyncrasy, I mentally reread great short stories, rethink Hitchcock movie endings, and re-examine what pretty girls say to me.

Two nights ago, I reread the short story entitled <u>Red</u> by W. Somerset Maugham. The plot was that he found his Eve as in the Garden of Eden at an island in Samoa. Just as life was totally blissful, <u>Red,</u> the main character in the story gets shanghaied and finds himself drugged and carried off to a tramp cargo ship steering for far off lands.

I recall the story that Red woke up and realized he was shanghaied and that life for him changed completely. Somehow, I was thinking of Red's dilemma when my own head ached, and I seemed to have transcended to another mind set. It went through my mind that what happened to Red was now happening to me. As my waking eyes regained most of their focus, I canceled my shanghaied notion because I saw that I was not on a ship, but on a couch in someone's house. I didn't recognize the house and tried to reconnect with the last thoughts which I could recall.

I remembered that very early in the day, I had to go to a very large Big Box hardware store. I purchased what I needed and decided that on such a sunny day, I would walk the tree lined neighborhoods that surrounded the location of the Big Box store.

After walking a few blocks I heard a voice say, "Mister, do you have a minute?"

I turned around and saw a lady behind a white picket fence where she was working in her garden. She stopped gardening and approached in order to ask me a question.

"Do you think the blue plants should be in front of the red ones, or does it matter?"

I looked at the nice looking, slim lady who was surrounded by potted plants in black plastic container cans. She was busily digging holes in the soil with a shovel. I saw her look up at me, and she repeated her question about how she should to locate the plants so that they would be arranged properly. My response was,

"If I'm not mistaken, the blue plants are Lantana, and the red ones are Impatiens. Impatiens do not do well in full sun. Lantana is a full sun plant, so plant the Lantana near the fence, and the Impatiens in the shade of the trees".

She went over to a can containing the red Impatiens' plants and found a plastic stick which indicated that they should be planted in partial sun.

"Say, you are right. I'll plant the Lantana in the front and the red ones under the trees".

She was now standing directly in front of me and only the fence separated us. She asked if I could use a cup of coffee or tea.

"Why not?" I thought.

She opened the fence gate for me, and we entered her house. The inside of her house was exquisite: A grand piano, oil paintings, and sofas and chairs of high quality. We went into her Sunset Magazine kitchen, and she asked again what she could make for us. I requested tea, and she had me select a tea bag from the mahogany caddy. She told me that her name was Carol. She was retired and had several bouts of arthritis in her shoulder joints. Gardening was what her physician recommended for her instead of pain-killer pills.

She said that her son told her to ease her arthritis by smoking marijuana. She told me that she tried smoking it but inhaling it made her sick. Her son then gave her a recipe for making Carrot Cake with pot as one of the key ingredients. Making carrot cake according to her son's recipe seemed to help her. It was also easy to consume. She said that she experienced no negative effects, and it helped ease her arthritis pains. She brought her cake and served me a piece and took a large slice of carrot cake for herself. We chatted for about an hour, and I enjoyed the tea, cake, and a large slice of cake.

All of a sudden, I became dizzy and groggy, and she steered me to a back yard couch. I fell asleep. But, where was I now? I was in a room with the black shades pulled down on the windows. I heard the telephone ring in the other room. I heard a man's voice talking to someone on the phone. Am I in trouble? Are they calling for a doctor? I stood up and made myself walk to the door. A man, a stranger to me, was still on the telephone. He was a burley young man. I didn't recognize the rooms of that house. Where was I? Who the hell was he? He motioned to me that he would only be a minute more on the phone. I looked out the front windows, and I was in a part of town that had no familiarity to me.

When he got off the phone, he gave me some bromo-seltzer in a big glass of water and told me his name was Winfield, or "Win" as he was known to most people. In the conversation that ensued, I realized that he was not a modern day shanghaier. He was Carol's pot smoking son who had been called to get me out of her backyard. We were now at his house. He knew all about me because he had gone through my wallet. However, nothing was missing from it.

Winfield told me the town I was in and that he was willing to take me to where I had left my car. I was anxious to get back home and deal with my head since it seemed to be in shadow land. I told him where I parked my car, and Winfield drove me there.

As I was ready to leave his pick-up truck, he said, "You leave my mother alone. Forget her. Don't try to go back to her house or there will be negative consequences for you".

I had no intention to eat more carrot cake. I zipped home and reviewed the happenings of the day. From then on, I'm going to be more knowledgeable and careful about the kind of carrot cakes made at home. How can something so delicious be so powerful?

In re-thinking the events of that carrot cake day, the more I'm convinced that I was shanghaied by my own expectancies of having a good time!

UNMASKING MR. SUTTER

As Marisol opened her front door, she immediately knew what had happened. She was totally more frightened than angry. Maybe it was lucky we had been away. She ran to the side of the house where Hernan, her husband, was unpacking the suitcases and souvenirs from Oahu.

Hernan ran to the front door and confirmed that during their vacation, they had been robbed. Gone was their entire living and dining room furniture. As he went through the house, he saw that the television, their bedroom, and Marisol's jewelry were not disturbed. He was about to report the robbery to the police when he discovered a note strapped to the telephone. The note was written on the outside of a large-sized envelope. It read as follows:

"I'm sorry that I have inconvenienced you.

I only took what I needed. I'm leaving you

sufficient money to pay for what I took.

Please don't call the police.

Hernan knew he should call the police, except that Marisol said,

"Stop. Wait a minute. Let's talk about this. If we call the police, they are going to keep the money as evidence, and we will have to wait a long time to refurnish. We will have to live months and even years without needed furniture. There is enough cash here that we can easily replace what went out the door. I think we don't call the police".

"Marisol, let's go through the house and see if we can figure out how the thieves entered the house".

Both of them looked throughout the house. There was no sign of a break-in. The chances were that either the back or front door was opened by the use of a plastic credit card slipped between the lock mechanisms and door frame. Neither door had an additional lock to secure them with a sliding bolt mechanism.

Both Hernan and Marisol made a list of what needed to be purchased. The locksmith was called immediately to re-key the existing locks and install the bolt mechanisms on the entry ways. When they went to town to purchase furniture for their two vacant rooms, they saw a sign that there was a 35% store-wide sale. In three days, every item that had been stolen was replaced. They now had better furniture and an additional thousand dollars of the money left them by the thief.

Hernan and Marisol felt that the quiet life they had lived needed an additional spark in order not to age before their time. They were in good health and enjoyed their prosperity but needed additional activities so that their brains could be geared to new rhythms. Hernan took a part time job as a cashier in a grocery store in town. Marisol answered a want ad in the local newspaper. The advertised job was to work as a housekeeper for a few hours during weekdays.

When Marisol talked to the man who needed a housekeeper on the phone in order to obtain the particulars of the job and to ascertain its location, it sounded like the perfect job. She could tell that the person who she talked with was well educated. When she arrived at his house, about three miles from where she lived, he answered the door. She was shocked because his face was so disfigured.

"Sorry to have shocked you", he said. "I am not contagious. If I scare you, be honest with me. I'll pay your wages for today and you need not return to put up with my hideous appearance".

"Mister Sutter, you did scare me, but as a housekeeper, I will be dealing with the house. You do not frighten me".

When she entered his house, a second shock almost brought her to her knees. There, in front of her, was the furniture she formerly had in her house. She didn't know how to react. Was Mr. Sutter a criminal? A man who could hurt her?

Mr. Sutter sensed that she had some hesitancy but didn't know the reason why she became more awkward as she entered his house. He said,

"Mrs. Gomez, let me explain my condition and myself to you. You are probably curious about me. My mother and father were normal in their appearances. I was born with some facial disfigurement and birthmarks and also with Vitiligo on my face and body. I lost my chance to be loved at birth. I had to be individually schooled by tutors who my parents knew. While I may look older, I'm forty.

I have written two novels about romance and lovers. I guess I extracted what I know about those subjects from books and radio programs. Now I have to vicariously understand what others say and do. How thrilling the pull of another can be. I can only seek your friendship because of the good people you are. Maybe you can help me sort out my thoughts in my next novel. I just read books to point me in the direction of what romance and love are in their profound stages".

Mr. Sutter made Marisol forget her fright and pity as she listened to his practiced explanation. He was who he was and through no fault of his own. Marisol accepted to do his housework, cooking, and obtaining the provisions he needed from town. Occasionally, Marisol would drive Mr. Sutter through the countryside in his automobile which had darkly tinted windows aside from the windshield. On such occasions, he described to her the names of the trees, flowers, the birds, and the nature of men on Harley Davidsons or red convertibles.

Marisol told her husband all that happened at work. The new tidbits that had been previously missing in their life augmented their conversation. Marisol allowed that it was out of his character to have taken their furniture, unless there was a greater mystery which she could not see or guess. Hernan came up with the idea of inviting Mr. Sutter to dinner at their house.

Marisol extended their dinner invitation to Mr. Sutter. He thanked her and said he would not be good company.

"That's a very poor excuse", Marisol responded.

A day later, he asked if he could change his mind and accept going to her home for dinner. Marisol left her car at his house and drove his car to her house.

When Mr. Sutter entered her house, he went into the living room and looked around. He appeared to be in a questioning mood. He then excused himself, and went outside the house and took a good look at it. He returned to state, "I've been here before".

"Hernan responded, "Oh tell us what makes you think you were at our house before".

"I'm so embarrassed and sorry that I was the person who robbed you of some furniture. What furniture you have here is in very good taste. I hope that the money I left you was sufficient to purchase such fine furniture. If it isn't, please tell me because I will gladly give it to you. Surely you can readily see why I couldn't go to jail. I would not last long amongst other convicts. I'm already in your debt because you didn't report the robbery. I guess I shouldn't stay for dinner now that you have found me out".

"Mr. Sutter, I am certain that you had your reasons for taking our furniture. In truth, you bought it from us. Anyway, you are our dinner guest and we'll talk as friends. We are glad that you are here. Can we start with a drink?

What would you like"?

"A double scotch is what I need now".

"Great! Coming right up".

"I saw that your mail box was full of mail and your place was in darkness for several days. When I remembered that the next day was Halloween, the idea formed in my head that I could go into the world and be accepted as abnormal on that day. As you know, I only have driven myself around the area at nighttime. For me, darkness is friendlier than daylight.

During my evening break from boredom, I drove around and noticed your corner mailbox was still overflowing. I took the chance you would not be home on Halloween. Therefore, I thought I would address the needs I had for some furniture that did not come with the purchase of my furnished home. I went to the U Haul rental place and robbed you of what I needed. All this I did because I have learned that for me person to person transactions have always backfired. I ask for your forgiveness.

Hernan, Marisol tells me you are taking a trip to Monterrey and Carmel this weekend. She also told me that I needed to get a mini oven to facilitate my warming up the meals that she makes for me. My question is, should I take your oven and leave some money, or will you help me get one from the store"?

"Mr. Sutter, you are now our friend. No need to hide from us. We will be glad to make any purchases that you need or want".

"May I have another double scotch"?

TROUBLE WITHIN

Laura and Lena were comfortable with each other until both began to like Sidney. A distance was created between them when Sid took Laura to his senior class prom.

Going to the prom with Sid was not unexpected by anyone other than Lena. Sid and Laura had been dating for some six months and seemed to be in each other's company on a regular basis. The fact that Lena didn't attend the prom was the root of their problems. In addition, Lena who had never been in Sid's company, did not stop her from liking him and wanting also to be with him. Lena's thought was that her sister, Laura, should have arranged that some dates included the three of them. After all, some twins share the same friend without having to quarrel about being so possessive and exclusive.

It was on prom night that Laura agreed to have sex with Sid. The scene for the sexual encounter was accomplished in Sid's garage in the back seat of his 1955 Mercury that was parked there. The romantic affair was planned in advance so that measures were taken to protect Laura.

When Laura arrived home, Lena immediately accused her of using her body to insure that Sid would only look at her. Lena scolded Laura.

"You're not in love with him. You just want to use your body to keep him interested. You probably will spoil his future by running away with him, instead of allowing Sid to go to College. I'm not going to tell Mom on you because you are my sister, but you should be reminded that you're a bad sister to me".

Laura knew enough about Lena's wants that she didn't reply to her ridiculous accusations. She factually told her:

"Lena, I'm not going to discuss Sid or my relations with him with you. Find yourself someone to be with other than the persons who are friends of mine".

With Lena, no advice or suggestions ever worked. Lena was always ready to do whatever was on her mind. She had always been a little competitive. This new display of anger was relatively new.

When Laura had one of her regular headaches, she took the medicine that calmed her pain but which made her have some anxiety issues. With Laura taking her medication for her headache and being numbed by it, it was time for Lena to become aggressive in carrying out a plan she had thought of to show up her sister.

She went over to Sid's house and rang the doorbell. He answered and was delighted to see the girl who he thought was Laura. He said,

"Hi, Laura, my folks are not going to be home until six o'clock. Come in".

Lena didn't mind being mistakenly called "Laura". It just made things easier for her. As expected, the question of "what do you want to do" came up. They went into Sid's bedroom and Lena undressed and jumped into Sid's bed before Sid had a chance to put his rubber on. Lena was incredibly turned on and frightened Sid with the number of orgasmic squeals that she uttered.

It was all over within an hour. Lena had accomplished her objective. She dressed and gave Sid his final kiss, left and returned home.

Lena didn't say anything to her sister. She just seemed happy and that in itself gave Laura the suspicion that something was wrong. Lena's actions on visiting Sid's house were soon discovered because Sid was left in a state

of euphoria. He telephoned Laura and told her how much he loved her and what a wonderful surprise her visit was for him. Laura quickly understood that her headache had been the opportune time for Lena to take advantage of her. Laura didn't like Sid's exuberant praises concerning the afternoon time and hung up on him.

"He can go to hell if after all this time, he can't tell the difference between me and Lena".

Lena had heard Laura talking to Sid and hanging up the phone on him. Lena knew that there would be no peace between them for a long while. Laura told Lena that she wasn't very clever and was a hypocrite for calling her "the bad sister". Laura told Lena that they would stop speaking to each other from that moment on.

Laura put two lined composition books on the table in their room. Those books were to write down whatever messages they had for one another. Lena just brushed off the idea of writing down her thought and complaints. "Just you wait, Laura, until you get your next headache. Wait and see what happens".

Laura wrote in her composition book how desperate Lena was to attract friendships. She wrote that she thought Lena had a real dark side and that she should tell her working single Mom to take her to a doctor for help.

Sid was confused at Laura's behavior and couldn't understand how she asked to be laid and then hours later had the phone hung upon him. He decided to get to the bottom of the change in behavior and rang Laura's doorbell. Laura opened the door and told him to go away. He was no friend of hers. Why had he made love to her sister?

"You're just one horny louse of a guy. No one else would do such a thing".

Laura then slammed the door and went to the bathroom to cry.

Sid was not only left with his mouth open in confusion, but also couldn't put Laura's inferences into any context.

Sid knew Jimmy Depp and his sister, Marion, who lived next door to Laura. He decided to first talk with Jimmy who, up to that time, only had considered Jimmy to be a recluse. He caught up with Jimmy and Marion at the public swimming pool he knew they frequented on Saturdays.

"Hey, Jimmy, have you ever seen Laura's sister?"

"No, I didn't know she had one", Jimmy answered.

Marion, who overheard the question, said,

"Sid, Laura is an only child. I've known her all my life".

"Oh, gosh, what have I gotten myself into"?

Sid then marched off to college, not wishing to see Laura anymore.

PRIMITIVES IN TODAY'S WORLD

Dr. Barker, a cultural anthropologist, came up with the theory, that some of the aborigines of the coastal to mid-highlands of Papua, New Guinea, were ready for change and eager to tap into some of the innovative amenities of the 20th and 21st centuries.

He thought that the solution for addressing change in their culture was to collect a cadre of capable persons he gathered at his Port Moresby office to implement his grant. He had interviewed the persons he called to implement ideas contained in his grant. I was one of the persons selected to fulfill the parameters of Dr. Barker's grant. While I had some trepidations in volunteering for such out-of- the way assignment, I told myself that I had been successful teaching in Thailand and was ready for a new challenge.

Arriving at Dr. Barker's bungalow office and looking around at the other persons who sat in a semi-circle around the professor's desk that he sat upon, my instinctive trepidations returned. Dr. Barker, himself, blinked his eyes a lot and had a mild stammering speech problem. When he started his introductions, that's when my stomach churned. The first person the professor introduced was a dark-skin man with an unusual hair-do or perhaps it was a massive wig. He was Huchi-Hutai, a Huli tribesman, who knew some English and would be most helpful in forming the language chain needed to communicate with the aborigines that had agreed in advance to welcome us to their tribal village as teachers.

Seated next to the tribesman was a man who grew up in the western equatorial jungles of Peru, Mr. Flecha Mendoza. He had expertise in herbal and homeopathic medicines. He also was knowledgeable in transmitting our communications on a short-wave radio. The introduction of a young Filipino lady who had previously taught at outback schools in Australia was Miss Corazon Bustamante. I sat next to her, and I was introduced as a former Peace Corps teacher who taught English to the Thais at an elephant reserve. My name is Viggo Ayres.

On the other side of me was a large woman wearing a strange, old fashioned riding outfit with jodhpurs. The strange outfit seemed to double her size. The only thing missing in her get-up was a horse to sit upon. Her name, Pricilla Putts. The last member of the group was the professor's step-son, a lad from Wyoming. His name was Jack Bushley. He had no experience outside of serving two years in the U.S. Army. Our mission was to teach English, and introduce writing and reading skills. We were also charged to help convey acceptable hygiene practices.

After a week of planning our mission to the more northern part of Papua where our Huli village was located, we embarked to travel there with our guides Huchi-Hutai and Flecha. They were familiar with the intricate landscapes we needed to traverse. We went by land rather than take a helicopter because the native tribesmen thought the whirlybirds were a bad omen because of how they disrupted nature. During the four days of travel and camping, I marveled how Pricilla kept herself attired in her boots and ballooning riding outfit. Evidently, she must have had several similar outfits with her because what she wore always seemed fresh. The part of the trip which was great was that we had no schedule to adhere to for our arrival; therefore, we were able to pace ourselves. During our journey, Pricilla took over because she had a commanding voice and didn't mind telling everyone what she thought and also volunteered herself to set tasks for everyone, every time we camped.

When we arrived at our Huli village, our quarters consisted of two Quonset huts that once served as a military outpost constructed to obtain information that could be used to defend Papua from any Japanese attack in WW II.

Arriving at our tribal village, Pricilla told us who was to sleep where. Flecha, Jack, and I would sleep in the smaller hut. Huchi already had his own piece of ground. Corazon and Pricilla were to sleep in the hut closest to the locked private outhouse. The furnishings consisted of cots with a rubber mattress, a large table, and fifteen folding chairs. Hammocks were also available.

Pricilla made Jack and me feel somewhat wimpy because of her loud voice and habit of hitting things with her riding crop as she talked to us and used it to give emphasis at group meetings. Huchi and Flecha didn't give her the attention she demanded of us and they generally came to discuss issues with me or Jack.

The gatherings to teach the natives were not well attended. They were more interested in holding on to their own customs. On special occasions, they painted their faces with a yellow-green paste. The men had bones ornamenting their noses and other feathered objects everywhere. The women were bare breasted and had all sorts of ornaments in their hair, faces, and private parts. The children were raised by the tribe after they gave up long time nursing of one or two years. The main meals consisted of sweet potatoes and, about once a week, pigs supplemented their limited supply of food.

All of us took our vitamin pills and partook of the feasting when pigs were roasted. The dancing at festivals was too erotic for us with the exception of Pricilla who tapped her riding crop to the rhythm of their drumming. The flute-like instruments and drum beats resulted in all the tribesmen hopping up and down in place. Apparently, that was the only dance they knew. Corazon and Jack usually stayed away from these feasts. These rites had war-like implications and invited a kind of out- of- body experience. These simulated throwing spears at an invisible enemy which engendered an aggressive attitude that made me feel most uncomfortable.

Huchi was always in his element during such special occasions. Thank goodness for the roasted pigs that helped sober the elders from their dancing frenzy. Swaying breasts didn't seem to bother Pricilla or me. I just saw it as a phenomenon that primitives down play nakedness. Peeking penises coming free from their loin cloths did not have any special effect on Pricilla. She was a matter-of-fact person that expressed her philosophy of "let it be" and summed it up as,

"We have to take things as they are and never interfere with cultural rites. We are not missionaries".

Huchi communicated with Flecha that one of the most influential tribesman's wife was having a difficult time giving birth. The tribal chief and the shaman asked Flecha to help. Flecha responded after he picked up his specially equipped Red Cross Kit. He followed Huchi to where the woman was in labor and could see that she was suffering and in great pain.

Flecha understood her problem and asked Huchi to get Pricilla. Pricilla responded immediately. She rubbed mineral oil over the top of the baby's head that was half-way out and hoped that Flecha did not need to make an incision since Flecha was uncertain how to have such a cut heal. However, with the help of Pricilla holding down the patient, she was also able to help push to free the large-headed baby into the world. Pricilla seemed to know how to help the mother. Later she told Flecha that it was the first time that she had ever participated in such an ordeal and had never even witnessed a birthing previous to that day's complicated delivery.

The tribesmen also celebrated and killed pigs for the feast that was to follow. Again, Corazon and Jack left when the tribesmen became intoxicated and gave us sinister looks. Jack had decided that he was never going to be able to be a cultural anthropologist like his step-dad. At the feast, Pricilla and I held our ground and dismissed the jumping- in-place dances and the chanting that we anticipated would become a frenzied ritual that ended only when some tribesmen retired to eat and others to have sex.

The day after such an exhaustive evening by all of us in camp, our team decided to spend time at a meeting to figure out if we should continue remaining at this locale or to regroup at Port Moresby with Dr. Barker to explain the fact that we were not having much of an effect on teaching the tribesmen in the areas that we had been charged to do. By the end of the meeting, Pricilla made her points emphatically. We were still regarded as strangers – perhaps even as aliens. It was too soon to cut and run. We decided to remain there and work more on a person-to-person basis.

Actually, Pricilla gave us good advice. Things improved in a better way for a while. It was only when the tribesmen painted their faces and polished their pierced nose bones and fixed their massive hair wigs that it was best to keep out of the way of the Huli tribesmen.

The everyday problem that we encountered was that scheduling events for us was a haphazard undertaking because time itself was not a concept that they understood. Our team was the only ones who knew about clocks and watches or summoning whistles; otherwise the natives would show up for our activities on a walk-in basis.

One fruitful day we had our events for the day thwarted when some highland Hulis came to visit. They were painted in face and body, feathered, nose-boned, fierce, and a few had human heads attached to poles. We had nothing to defend ourselves. Flecha had our only machete. The machete was no match for the weaponry being exhibited by our visitors. Luckily, the tribes exchanged a few females and the visiting tribesmen left peacefully.

Since the exchanging of females was an established custom, we had no say and took no part to express our disapproval. Pricilla explained her idea to us as to the reason this was an important practice and probably had the salutary effect of protecting their small tribe against inbreeding. Huchi could not understand the gist of the questions put to him for an explanation. On the other hand, Flecha voiced the idea that we were lucky they didn't see Corazon. Jack spoke up and said that he had locked her in the outhouse when the visiting warriors were in camp. Jack expressed his desire to leave as soon as possible.

Flecha reported how all our group was in jeopardy to the person on the other end of our radio broadcasts. That far-away radio operator acknowledged that we were on borrowed time and that he would convey our problem to Dr. Barker. Dr. Barker quickly responded that he was able to send a helicopter ready to evacuate us if we voted unanimously to leave our camp.

Any use of a helicopter was a gamble in that it would upset the tribesmen. They continued to believe that the helicopter was the bearer of bad omens that could spread diseases and swarmed insects. When the call from the tribe's powerful shaman came to Flecha, he and Huchi were asked to respond to another medical problem. This time, it was another woman who was having excessive convulsions and screaming because she couldn't give birth. Flecha had seen the problem of breach births in livestock. He never knew that such occurrences also happened in humans. Flecha called upon Pricilla for advice. Pricilla shook her head and asked,

"What did you do with the llama that you saved"?

Flecha explained that even with large animals, the task was very intricate. With a human, dealing with a breech birth could prove deadly for both the mother and the baby. He wanted to back away, but the on-looking tribesmen pointed their spears at Flecha and Pricilla.

"Flecha, you must try or she will die, and it will be interpreted that we were unwilling to treat her".

Flecha thought he could try to get advice from a Port Moseby physician, but he wasn't allowed to leave the screaming woman. Pricilla told Flecha,

"There's no time. She has to be helped immediately. Let me sponge your hands and arms with peroxide and you repeat the procedure that you did for the llama".

Flecha washed as the aching woman passed out. Pricilla kept encouraging Flecha to keep turning the baby so that the head would be moved into its proper position. When the baby was pulled into the world, Pricilla could see that it had an off-color and was extremely weak. The woman was still breathing but was also in jeopardy of failing to recover. It was explained to Huchi that the baby needed to be given to a surrogate mother because the birth mother was too weak.

When Flecha and Pricilla returned to the big hut, Huchi followed. He said,

"Tribesmen don't like what you did. They very angry. We better leave".

An hour later, the shaman and others came to get Flecha. They dragged him to a pole that usually held whatever target the tribesmen tied to the post to practice hitting it with their spears. Immediately, Pricilla shouted at the tribesmen that were holding Flecha. She yelled at them,

"No, no! Get away from him. I'll take care of him".

Huchi was trembling. Miraculously, the tribesmen let go of Flecha. Pricilla jumped on his back and whispered something into his ear as he fell to the ground on all fours. Pricilla mounted him and struck him again and again with her riding crop. Flecha screamed with pain. The gathered tribesmen all backed away bewildered at such goings on. The extraordinary never-before-seen drama had the tribesmen looking at each other, and seemingly asking

"What's going on"?

Finally, Flecha crawled to the Quonset hut with Pricilla still whacking him. Once inside the hut, Pricilla told Flecha to get on the radio and then she told the rest of us to pack up. Flecha asked,

"Why did you hit me so hard? I would have yelled like you told me to without the hurt you inflicted".

"Don't be silly. These guys know pain. They also know when it is not administered. Let's get busy".

The call was made to the operator at Port Moseby. The helicopter would be on its way in minutes. Huchi came to tell everyone that while the tribesmen were afraid of Pricilla, the mother and baby were fading away. Should either or both die, the tribesmen would regroup and come to take revenge on their killers. The jumping up and down was about to start when the noise of the black whirlybird distracted the tribesmen. The helicopter scooped down near a level area next to the Quonset huts. With all aboard, including Huchi, they left the primitive encampment. Dr. Barker was disappointed that his idea didn't get implemented but the notoriety given his failed experiment was celebrated in various media sources. That in itself pleased him immensely.

When I went back to get a better look at the botanical gardens and trees, plants, and flowers, an Indian man came up to me and asked,

"Have you seen that big lady that's walking in her horsey outfit? What a nut! Who but a crazy person would wear such ridiculous clothes in this awful heat".

I answered him,

"Sir, you are judging the lady by her cover. You are not accurate in your assessment of her. She is not a nut. If it's who I think you are referring to, she is the greatest human being I have ever met. I owe my life to her. Be thankful that persons like her still exist"!

When I heard the sound of the words that I directed at the turban-clad man, I reflected on the aspects of what I said.

"Where is my common sense"? I asked myself.

I hurried along the paths of the garden and caught up with Pricilla.

"Pricilla, our surroundings are so much better here than what we had in the wild. Do you have time to go to tea with me?"

"Yes, but wouldn't it be nice to make it High Tea so we can tell each other what we don't know about ourselves"?

"High tea, it is."

OUT- OF-WORK BOOK-MARKS

The stiff blue paper book-mark was idle for two days after the high school teenager had finished "The Old Man and the Sea". It was now in the small top drawer of his bureau.

The book-mark was the kind of marker that liked to work. It didn't like being discarded into the darkness of the drawer with hope that the drawer would only be its temporary cell. Its short stay in the dark drawer had it reviewing the last story in which it had worked.

When the drawer was pulled open, the blue book-mark thought it might have another book assignment. That was not the case. The drawer closed. Darkness returned. An additional problem was created when a wrinkled all green book-mark was put into the drawer. Quickly, the blue book-mark regretted its luck because the green book-mark was now in a frontal position and would probably be in line to go to work before it. When the Green book-mark asked if its neighbor had been there long, a more optimistic outlook infused Blue. Ah…. It had Green to share thoughts with and no longer needed to be completely alone and bored.

"Were you ever in a book" asked Green?

"Why, yes. I was in a book about an old Cuban fisherman. He was born to fishing. He knew how to catch fish but, in recent times, Santiago was having bad luck".

"Blue, was the story of old Santiago a good read"?

"Oh, yes, but you know how it is. A lot of the story was missed because I was never allowed to witness all the thoughts that appeared in the story. But I could tell it was a good read because one of his teachers assigned it to him for summer reading".

"Blue, since we now have no employment as markers, tell me about that old fisherman".

"I am almost certain that old Santiago was symbolic of man's struggles with his own inside and outside energies. Ernest Hemingway made it apparent that the old man was challenging the marlin, the sea, life, and himself.

When hooked, the huge black marlin leaped high out of the water to show himself to the old man. It was at that moment that Santiago began his philosophical conversations and fight with what the King of Fish represented to him.

'To where are you pulling my boat? Do you think I'll cut my line because you are taking me far from land? I may be old, but I've been made ready for you by the elements and the way I have been bumped about in order to stay alive. I don't know for sure but, most likely, you must have had it easier than I have had to endure the deep ruts in life. We will soon find out which one of us has enough fight to determine who is better able to survive. I do know that no independent creature survives without being tested time and time again. Although we're both puny in this vastness, we are here and I will win and you will have to yield to me.

You have pulled me away from land for two days and now I see that you are weakening. As much as my muscles ache, my calloused, unwashed bloody hands will guide you to my launch'.

The magnificent marlin tried to go to the deep, but the pull of Santiago's line play prevailed. The giant fish was moved to the side of the boat. His catch proved to be larger than his boat. To make the kill, the beautiful fish had to be harpooned. The blood from his wounds began to leave its trail as the old man turned the boat around to row home.

Green, it was not long before the Makos swarmed. The sharks took turns at dining on the huge fish that was secured to the side of the boat. Santiago killed a few sharks but ....".

"But, what? What happened, Blue"?

"I was removed when the young man put me down and finished the book. I can only guess that Santiago won one struggle to encounter a more hopeless situation. This, too, happens in life for persons that get into aging without pesetas. So, here I am, waiting and waiting for my teenager to read another book."

"Well, such is the problematical work we are in. But what you related makes me glad, as a Blue book-mark, to know one more story. You want to hear what the kid had me in"?

"Yes, what story did you manage to bridge"?

"The last paperback book into which I was inserted was a story about a guy who is committed to a state psychiatric hospital for the insane, a Cuckoo's Nest. McMurphy is comfortable in being who he is, a non-conformist. He will be in immediate trouble at the hospital because he is bound to rebel against the established regulations that are in place. The fact is that the regulations were imposed by ex-military nurse, Nurse Ratchet.

At first, McMurphy sees Nurse Ratchet as a woman who may be in need of compliments. He soon learns that she happens to stand for rigid rules instead of any displays of feminism. McMurphy quickly assesses that the "carrot approach" is useless; therefore, he decides to become influential with his colleagues by approaching the nurse's rules by using the "stick" approach.

He manages to lead his peers in a series of hijinks capers. Through manipulation, McMurphy illegally procured a bus. He takes the entire group of patients on a real fishing expedition. Their enormous bliss is ended when they are returned to their hospital facility. McMurphy's psyche cannot be changed through punishment. Punishment is the expected remedy when he challenges rules or laws. The last straw for Nurse Ratchet is that over a weekend when she is not on duty, McMurphy uses his contacts on the outside to bring in a prostitute to address a young inmate's male virginity status. While that caper takes place, booze flows throughout the large common suite of the psychiatric ward.

Upon the return of Nurse Ratchet, she is wounded to the core. She knew instinctively that the chaos she witnessed was concocted by her nemesis, McMurphy. The retribution was in her court. The power for decision making was certified by her position. The remedy for McMurphy's transgressions was that his way of being had to be curbed permanently. A lobotomy was his punishment for making his peers happier persons. McMurphy was transformed into a vegetable state. His former assertiveness and thinking process were now history.

His most devoted friend, a huge and powerfully built American Indian who McMurphy had christened "Chief", assessed his friend's predicament and instinctively knew that he was now made to be an empty container. The day the Chief realized what had been done to his pal, the Chief took his pillow and smothered McMurphy. The Chief now was a changed person because of the influence made on him by McMurphy. Chief escaped into the world never to return to any form of institution. The weaker inmates returned to their former existence."

"Blue, this is what I think: McMurphy left his mark in the time he had the upper hand, but so did the evil Nurse Ratchet. McMurphy managed to be the one who "Flew Over the Cuckoo's Nest". Nurse Ratchet was left to walk the world in deep sea diver's shoes. I believe Ken Kesey who wrote the story of "One Flew Over the Cuckoo's Nest" probably was telling us that some abnormalities are acceptable to society, and others are unacceptable. Normal persons are packaged with approved abnormalities.

Many persons cannot tell which abnormality is a minus or a plus. We usually don't examine how or why persons are given labels such as "okay to roam" or "better lock the bugger up". In re-thinking, the Chief understood that in this case, the "nuts" were in charge of the psychiatric hospital's wards. Blue, isn't that a good story"?

"Green, I can't wait until our high school teenager puts us to work again. We both love stories. Let's hope we go to work soon."

Suddenly, the drawer opened and hope was renewed by the thought of working again!

IT'S FOR MY JENNY

His circle of friends was speechless when Tomas told them he was going to marry Jenny Dos Pasos. They recovered to ask: "why"? When Tomas stared at them one by one, their eyes returned continued bewilderment.

His answer was that they're not using their brains. They were being influenced by female movie actresses, magazine covers, the high five ladies at our favorite tavern, and, therefore, in their current mental states they would not experience anyone that would give them a good morning greeting.

On the other hand, he had studied Jenny's attributes.

"Jenny is a nice person. She lives with her parents and goes to church every now and then. Ever since I've known her, she has been working as the hostess at the Blue Room at the St. Clair. She's younger than I by a year-and-a half and seems to enjoy prime health. I'm certain she will make a good marriage partner. She's intelligent. What else do you guys expect"?

Tomas' four best friends indicated that he was hasty and should continue to meet prettier girls.

"I am right about you guys thinking you ae going to marry your individual fantasies. Jenny is real and I'm marrying her on July 4th, so that we can sit back at Washington Park and have the city illuminate the sky with fireworks for us".

Tomas knew that what hadn't been said about Jenny was that she didn't flash her smile at any of them and was reserved in the presence of men.

On the morning of July 4th, Tomas Trujillo took Jenny Dos Pasos to be his wife at a German beer garden that was rented during its off-hours. Their wedding was a casual affair. Jenny was in a beautiful sack dress and Tomas had on his laundered and starched white dress shirt, tie, and Dockers black trousers. After all, his wedding indicated the affordable person he took himself to be. His circle of friends behaved themselves –maybe the wedding was early for them to act up. What made Jenny happy was that a number of the ladies connected to her place of work were very happy and lively as they danced to the tunes played on the tavern's jute box. Tomas lost his nervousness when he doubled down on his love commitment for Jenny.

After the beer garden, the newly-weds changed to more comfortable clothes and the entire wedding group wanted to continue to party. All endorsed at the idea of elongating the party and taking the ferry to Rupert Island. They were able to disembark with the understanding that other ferries would return them to the starting point.

On the island, Tomas stayed near the shoreline because it became known to Jenny and others that he was very susceptible to getting poison oak. He was also afraid of bees and had been told by his doctor that their sting was toxic and if stung, he needed to report immediately to be treated at a hospital.

The sea shore was breezy and the love for each other kept them warm and anxious to skip the fireworks and go to the apartment Tomas was rented. It was Jenny's suggestion to jump onto the next ferry that stopped at Rupert Island before anyone noticed and go home. Once home, nervousness returned to both. Without hesitation, Tomas told Jenny as she came from the bathroom in cotton pajamas,

"Jenny, take everything off. You are my wife, and I cannot wait for us to be nude together".

Morning came quickly, and Tom had to be at the bank by eight o'clock, since he was an assistant manager. Jenny had taken three days off to fix their apartment. Her normal shift at work was from three p.m. to eleven ll'clock. She told Tomas that he could dine at the Blue Room anytime he wished. Otherwise, they would see each other full-time on Sundays. These awkward arrangements for newly-weds were important to be made in that it would provide the surplus dollars needed for developing and meeting their future plans.

Jenny was a serious person. In quick time, she had the apartment painted, redecorated, bought a new queen size bed set and gave the windows a needed color treatment. Her retired parents provided many semi-valuable works of artwork to cover what had been bare walls and also bought her some nice throw rugs. The transformation of the apartment was done quickly and bewitched Tomas by its elegant appearance. Their irregular work hours were difficult to handle, but their savings account was acknowledged to be compensation for meeting future goals.

After Tomas and Jenny celebrated five years of marriage, Mr. and Mrs. Dos Pasos, Jenny's loving parents, thought their daughter was Mrs. Trujillo for the rest of her life. They presented Jenny and Tomas with a check for $200,000 so that they could make a sizeable down payment on a home. With the $200,000 from their own savings account, Jenny and Tomas bought a house. It was a wonderful home which was spacious and had a large basement and attic.

The Dos Pasos' were proud of their daughter and son-in-law. Mr. Dos Pasos, Jenny's father, was retired as a major in the National Guard. He was getting treatment for prostate cancer. Jenny's mother visited Jenny on Mondays because Jenny worked Tuesday through Saturdays. Their vaulting into a better home and a higher standard of living didn't change their routines or working conditions.

Their marriage appeared to be built on bedrock until about the seventh year when Tomas was promoted to bank manager at a larger more distant bank. The assistant manager at his new assignment was a beautiful blonde who wore designer clothes and looked spiffy in whatever she wore. She was the kind of lady that his friends of bachelor days thought he would marry.

When he married Jenny, he changed his course and lived the responsible life. He had been happy.

At a "Thank God It's Friday" office party, Stella sat next to him and changed his routine of going straight home. After work, Tomas and Stella drank and ate fish and chips in a pre-courting get-together. As Tomas laughed at the various comments Stella made about observations that members of the bank staff and some of the deeds of customers and nonsense seen on television or movies, he could foretell that a future affair between them was inevitable.

He barely made it home before Jenny came in the door at 11:30 p.m. She gave him her paycheck to be deposited at the bank, and they went to bed. It seemed to Jenny that her husband had an unknown perfume fragrance on his cheeks. His suit coat needed brushing. Blonde hairs were a sign of his closeness to someone at the bank's TGIF gathering. The same blonde hairs appeared and reappeared on his suits. Jenny didn't know what she should do or say to Tomas.

After hesitating to involve her mother by seeking her advice, she succumbed to have her woman-to-woman talk. Her mother provided wounded counsel. Her husband had once strayed but returned home to her a wiser person. That was the crux of the advice that Jenny received, along with the added suggestion that she say nothing to Tomas.

Jenny knew this was an unbearable situation and had counsel but she would try it out for a week. At the end of the week, Jenny decided to go to Tomas' bank. There, in front of Tomas' desk, sat a lady in an Armani suit. Her blonde hair gave her away. Her brand of perfume solidified the evidence about what tormented her and needed to be resolved. She left the bank in tears and without a word said to Tomas.

When she arrived at her parent's home, her father was having lunch at the kitchen table. Her red eyes were a giveaway to her dad. He hugged her and told her to sit down across from him and tell him the cause of her sadness. Her dad advised her to confront Tomas. Jenny knew she had to do this. When Tomas arrived home that evening, harsh words were said to each other. Tomas admitted to Jenny that he could not help himself. He had fallen in love with his blonde without meaning to do so. He wanted a divorce. Jenny told him to leave the house. He did so. She stayed to cry and cry.

The next day, her father called Jenny and the scenario of the night before was related to him with great precision. Her father told his daughter to come to their home to spend a few days and to see what would transpire. Three days later, her father asked her to call Tomas and tell him the coast was clear for him to go to his house and pick up whatever he needed. Tomas agreed to go there after work.

After work, Tomas went to the home which he and Jenny had sacrificed to obtain. "Oh, well", he reasoned. He would still have a great deal of money since he would get half from the sale of their house. He went into his front door carrying a couple of suitcases. As he went into his bathroom, Tomas tripped on some unknown obstacle, and the bathroom door slammed. He looked in time to see the door knob turn and heard several clicking sounds on the outside of the bathroom door. The bathroom was windowless. The lights went out, and he was in darkness. The light switch was out of order. He couldn't walk without stumbling and fell again on what entangled his feet. Jenny must be playing a joke on him because there, on the bathroom floor, were some kind of bushes or vines. He remembered his cell phone light. When his cell phone lit, he saw that the floor was covered in poison oak bushes. Then, through the door, he heard the deep voice of his father-in-law asking,

"How are you doing, Tomas"?

"Please open the door", he yelled.

"Sorry. By the way, your cell phone will not work to call out. I cemented and wired the attic floor so your cell phone will not work in the bathroom. You are more in trouble than you realize. Look in the bath tub and see what your fate will be".

Tomas opened his cell phone to light and look into the bath tub. There in the bath tub was a beehive. Tomas could see the swarm of bees moving about. He quietly tried to turn the bathroom tub faucets so that he could drown the thousands of honey bees. The water had been shut off.

"Oh, please….open the door before I get stung".

"Sorry….."

"I love Jenny, and I'll not divorce her".

"Too late! You're locked in".

Tomas tried to use his cell phone to call 911. It didn't work. He banged on the door but only heard laughter.

"Hey, Tomas, I'm packing your suits, shirts, and shoes for you. I'm only leaving your pin-striped blue suit with a note to Jenny to give it to the undertaker. You will look good in it when you are in your coffin".

"Ouch! I'm getting stung. I'll be dead if you don't open this door".

"Now, you are getting the point. You're not leaving this house alive".

"Please….I beg you. Open the door! I have to get to a hospital. You will die with me because this is murder".

"Yes. This is murder. The way things are messed up in our courts, I don't think there will be time to put me on trial. You see, I'm turning myself in so that Jenny will be left out of having any part in being involved in my plan for you. My cancer is irreversible. I have only a week or two to live. I hope I have enough energy to discard the suitcases that I have filled with your clothes.

Good-bye Tomas".

WHAT GOES AROUND..................

I, Ponce Ramirez, grandson of the famous warrior and great Chief Osso of the Red Falcon people have written what my father remembers of that long reign. My understanding is that in Osso's early life, he was an activist as well as a fierce warrior.

Osso told my father that in his early years, he was wrong to do the many unworthy things that brought him fame as a warrior. When Osso became chief, he tried to make up for the traditional and culturally acceptable deeds performed by his people. As his thinking clarified, he thought of undertaking necessary changes in himself.

I, Ponce Ramirez, want to tell you about my grandfather, his ideas, his accomplishments, and stress the context of his time to you. Using my father's words, this is what and how he told me about my grandfather's life:

Before Osso became chief, Chief Nataku called upon us warriors to do whatever was his bidding. My father died in battle. My mother had many daughters and is without favor within the Red Falcon people. Her daughters aren't known to me as sisters since their father doesn't recognize me being in his family.

In the many summers that have passed, the Red Falcons have had the same shaman. He was Sukku, the shaman or witchdoctor of our tribe. During the time my grandfather was a fierce warrior, he still kept his contrary thoughts to himself about another way to live life. It was Osso's quest to find a way for his critical ideas to be voiced. He only had a few of his relatives who could let him voice his differences with chief Nataku. Nataku wanted to be rich and have young wives, animal hides, colorful bird feathers, weapons, and trophies of those who resisted the Red Falcon tribe in battle.

Nataku didn't care for Osso. It may be because of what he sensed about him or what the shaman has seen and reported about his reluctance to march on the neighboring tribes for the purpose of taking whatever they could use for their booty. Osso believed that taking what was prized by others kept the violated hating the Red Falcon tribe. Killing fathers, husbands, sons, and sometimes angry and resistant women and children seemed morally wrong to Osso. If Osso had not done his part in raiding other tribes and in having skills superior to his brothers, he would have been severely punished. Instead, Osso was praised by all who saw him in action.

In the last raid of the Mostasas campsite, the Red Falcons were able to capture several young and strong women. Amongst the captives was Corina, the very young wife of the chief of the Mostasas tribe who Osso killed. Since she was booty, Nataku ruled that Corina was for him to have as an exclusive servant. She must have been an exotic devilish prize because three weeks after taking her, old Nataku had a massive seizure and died two days later. Corina was claimed and passed on to Tooch who replaced Nataku as chief. The time of mourning caused unfriendly meetings for the circle of power. Tooch wanted to rid himself of Sakku, the old shaman who advised the former chief. This became dicey as the old medicine man had been rooted in the tribe for many years. Therefore, Sakku continued to swear allegiance and was kept on as the Chief's advisor.

When their disagreements were at midpoint, Tooch called Osso to his circle and told him he was his friend and that from that day on he could sit in his circle of power. This pleased Osso who declared his loyalty to Tooch. They both went for a walk away from the camp and Tooch told Osso that he wanted him to sleep with Corina. He wanted Osso to make certain that she didn't have the resource within her to expedite the chief's death. She was to be Osso's only until he cleared her and returned her to Tooch.

Osso had to prove his loyalty. He didn't understand that Corina would be any kind of a complication. However, that was not the case because Ilta, Osso's wife, cried and pushed him away. Osso had the shaman explain to her the temporary situation that Tooch ordered.

Corina accepted her role and knew that her life depended on her participation in whatever was demanded. She tried to make friends with Ilta and Osso's children, but Osso could tell that Corina was not given more status than that of a servant. Osso's discovery was that she had immense energy and tightened her body in so many ways that Osso thought he better limit his time in the dark with her.

At the circle of power, a story surfaced that had been told by a captive slave woman who was taken in a raid of the Mostasas. Her warrior master related the merits which she had described to him of her Mayonesa tribe. She was a young girl when she was taken captive by the Mostasas from the Mayonesas tribe. She told of how her tribe had beaver skins, horses, and many fish to eat. In re-telling what she had conveyed to her master, he relayed it to Chief Tooch who became interested in finding out where this woman, Wukka, had been captured by the Mostasas tribe. Questioning Wukka, she described her tribe's territory in detail and explained where her tribe's location was. She related that it took many days journey to reach the bountiful land where she grew up.

After it was determined that Wukka knew the directions which would take her home, Chief Tooch told Osso and two other brave tribal brothers to find out about the treasures described at the circle of power. If they couldn't find her tribe, or if her telling of the story was not accurate, Wukko was to be stoned. Osso and two brothers, plus Wukka, and Corina made ready for a long journey through the territories of many other tribes. Corina knew she would be in danger if she did not continue to be obedient. She was the same age as Wukka and was good company for Osso and Wukka.

They departed in late spring so as not to have to deal with snow or winter storms. As soon as they left, Wukka gave many evidences that she knew where she was headed. Corina and Wukka became close. Corina was well versed in making camp, preparing and cooking roots and game animals. The trip they were on was difficult and their small group had to travel carefully through previously unknown territories that had scattered other gatherings of native peoples. After two phases of the moon, they reached their destination.

Wukka had retained her language skills and explained who she was. Her parents identified her with passionate exaltation. They were welcomed because they said they came in peace and would only stay for a few days. Corina made no attempt to escape. She tried to convince Wukka to stay with her people. Wukka took her opportunity and hid in her parents' place until Osso's party left. The trails had been marked on the way up so that they could find their way back to their camp.

The three who went to the Mayonesa's campground met with the circle of power and declared that everything that Wukka had told them was accurate. There was a great river with fish that they dried and was good to eat. They had horses that they mounted and used to hunt big game. They had hides of horses and deer. The tribe had some weapons but they didn't seem to be ready to fight veteran warriors or be prepared in a surprise raid. Chief Tooch asked his circle for counsel,

"How many warriors can we spare for a full circle of moon so we can have more blankets, and horses to help us conduct future raids"?

The shaman indicated,

"You have to leave enough warriors here to defend us because our neighboring tribes shouldn't see us as being in a weakened condition. If they see us having fewer warriors and many women and children, they may raid us. You can only spare about twenty to thirty warriors. Can that few warriors travel and bring us back the riches you seek"?

Chief Tooch postponed his decision for a few days and announced,

"We will meet again in two evenings."

He called Osso and his two brothers to answer the question posed by the shaman. Osso told him that the only problem would be bringing back what they could carry. Tooch dismissed everyone with the exception of Osso in order to speak in private.

"You still look strong and healthy. I believe it's time for me to take back Corina. Have her come to me with all her possessions". Osso had to adhere to the bargain that was previously made concerning the exchange.

Twenty-seven of their warriors followed their previously marked trails. Their journey was less than ideal. They had trouble keeping everyone together and out of sight of other people's campgrounds. There were some other white-faced traveling groups during summer, and they also had to be skirted. It was difficult to add to the food supplies that they had at the outset of their march. They marched in hunger.

When they arrived at their destination, the village seemed smaller than Osso remembered. They could still see the horses and the shacks that were full of dried fish and had tiers of small canoes piled up. Osso decided to attack the Mayonesas encampment at dawn. That night, they watched them light fires and to squat in circles to eat and talk. Osso's group was in great need of food and decided to attack the Mayonesas while it was dark.

As they attacked, the Mayonesas' fires were put out as Osso's warriors attacked them in darkness. Osso's warriors were surprised and fought only minutes before deciding to abandon their raid because a large group of Mayonesa warriors attacked them from the rear. Osso's raiding party came away with only two prisoners and a horse. They had to quickly march home. Luckily, they were not followed.

After they tortured their two prisoners, they were able to piece what botched up Osso's raid. The evidence given was that Wukka had convinced her tribal leaders that Chief Tooch would send a raiding party to their encampment. They prepared to survive the raid by posting runners at a twelve-hour distances in order to forewarn their people as the raiding party grew near. Once warned by the runners, the Mayonesa warriors who had been hidden in the forest attacked from a rear position and surprised Osso and his fighters.

Reporting back to Chief Tooch and the circle of power, the disappointment was such that Chief Tooch had Osso punished. He blamed Osso for the defeat. Osso was tied to a nearby large tree and left there for the forest animals to inflict punishment.

That night, Corina cut him loose from the tree. She told Osso that Chief Tooch was very sick. They returned to their sleeping camp and entered the chief's quarters. They were about to carry him into the forest and tie him to the same tree from where Osso escaped. However, Chief Tooch was shaking and had a fever, and was moaning in pain. Osso went to get the shaman to attend to Chief Tooch. After some extreme shaking, Chief Tooch let out a low moan and stiffened. He was dead. The shaman told Osso that it was Corina who killed Tooch in the same way that she killed Nataku.

"Furthermore," he said, "Our chiefs are too old for her, and she caused them to have so much fun that it resulted in their having seizures".

Osso grabbed the shaman by the throat and told him if he repeated what he had just said that he would see to it that he no longer would belong to the circle of power council. The shaman seemed to agree and looked at Corina and made the gesture that his lips were zipped. The entire village camp began mourning rituals. They chanted and finally built his pyre and Chief Tooch's corpse became ashes. The circle of power council met and looked at Osso, asking him

"If you should be selected leader, what wisdom would you provide"?

Osso already had his ideas about how their tribe should be modified.

This is what Osso stated:

"I would retain the practicing of the skills for war just in case we are raided. I would not continue raiding other tribes. I would invite other chiefs to smoke with me and see if we could begin to prosper from not sacrificing ourselves in war. We should all keep all of our possessions and not invade each other's tribes to take what doesn't rightfully belong to us. Everyone should keep his own horses, maidens, and food supplies. We should spend our time learning to hunt, trap game, and fish the streams in spring and summer. We should focus on building a better village and a better life".

Hours later, the council made their decision. Although not yet very old, Osso was made their Chief. The only proviso was that he stop sleeping with Corina because they wanted Osso to implement the ideas he had voiced to them. It was agreed that Corina was to be returned to the Mostasas people – a tribe that was not too far away.

After seeing the dark side of hostilities, Osso became a benevolent ruler. Bliss lasted for a few years. Later, Sukku, the shaman, came to visit him in secret. Osso was told that there was a young buck named Totto who was talking about how silly Osso's leadership was being displayed. He knew that before the change to become a peace loving tribe, their chiefs used to be fierce and enriched themselves through their raids of other tribes. They advocated returning to how they used to be.

Osso told his shaman that it was too bad Corina had been sent away. He would give her to the young buck because with him around, Osso's other progressive inclinations were going to encounter trouble. No doubt Totto has some of the same aspirations that he, Osso, once had disagreeing about how the Chief ran the Red Falcon tribe.

In the meantime, he would not change his thoughts or ways of ruling his tribe. He surmised that he may not be the Chief in his old age. He had a plan to distract Totto.

Footnote: The foregoing is what I, Ponce, learned from my father. Needless to say Totto didn't make trouble. The Chief of the Mostasa people agreed to exchange Corina for a Red Falcon woman. Corina was given to Totto as his servant. When he made Corina his wife, Totto fell in line with Osso as time went on.

What goes around.............

MR. CARD- CARRYING AFICIONADO

He was a small man, about 5'6" and between 135 and 145 lbs. He was always in dapper attire. He was very careful as to what impression he made. He was always evaluating himself.

His laugh was high pitched and frequently covered up the fact that he needed time to think about the response that needed to be made. His walk was a practiced fast pace and, even a twenty-foot path to a secretary's desk was done at a very rapid walk. He believed he was very important and that everyone was waiting for him: "the oracle" to say something clever or wise.

His memory was very good and part of his assignment to the three secretaries in his office was to scan the latest editions of newly released books on education. Their task was to type the salient points made in books and transfer them on 3"x5" cards. These findings were highlighted in yellow so his source and page number could be used in case that he needed it as a reference. He placed these cards in his vest pocket for further study and to commit them to memory.

The cards became his new thoughts and would be put into his own words to make an impression that he was the "know it all" in the field of education. His delivery was animated and manipulated for maximizing his personality. He was surely a phony for he didn't have much of himself to offer. What there was of him were the roles he played

He was a play actor for the serious person. His up to date 3"x5" cards gave him the edge for being on top in the field of educational change. He combined what others said with his own promises for reform. He was a fountain of ideas that played well with the listeners who were hypnotized by his rehearsed cleverness. His Armani suits and designer tie, his manicured fingernails were much appreciated by all the ladies, especially those of the P.T.A.

He was the District Superintendent of Schools, and the adored educator of the members on the County Board of Education. He loved to talk about table settings, crystal collections, great art, opera, ballet and symphonic pieces. His views on cultural matters were learned from book outlines on 3"x5" cards.

He stated with conviction that things were improving as even when they slid in another direction. He was not bothered by real statistics or negative results. He was most willing to give out other statistics and facts which were contrived by his own sleight of hand. That's what worked for him because, wasn't he "the oracle" who knew all about research and trends in education? The fact that the mice were playing while the little kitten was distancing himself from schools didn't matter in terms of politics. He had his legions, and they marveled at his wit and astuteness, no matter whether his statements lacked accuracy or not. In all this time, he was the "dream" of the County Board of Education, while the schools were becoming rudderless ships.

He was a difficult man because he always asked,

"Who said that?"

He usually asked, "Did he write anything that has been published recently?"

Mr. 3"x5" Card was not willing to take recommendations from his staff. He had his library sources from which he quoted. His fault was that he didn't know how to implement ideas. He greeted people with:

"I like your necktie"! or "Is that a Gucci bag you're carrying"? or "Good taste costs no more, and that's what I tell my best friends."

His pomposity was extreme, and some persons with other backgrounds thought he was a wise politician. He was over fifty years old and had already lived two hundred years of experiences, according to his own version of reality.

While he beat his drums like a jungle messenger, he was whatever he thought was his ready audience. He was the queen ant and could withstand and solve all problems. The other ants, in a crisis grabbed eggs on the ant hill and attempted to save their colony. He was soaring and circling the landscape while the staff tried to make sense of what to do in the trenches.

It was when he was on his self- fantasized mountain summit that his reversal of fortune began. One day when he was on a speech junket, his secretary opened his mail. An anonymous letter was opened, and there, without script, was a photograph of Mr. Elegance dressed in a Chanel dress and with the accoutrements of lipstick, false eye lashes, powder and rouge.

His secretary quickly covered the photo with her hand and then with other mail to hide the photograph of Mr. 3x5. The redness of the secretary's cheeks gave her away to the others in the office. They wanted an explanation for her ruffled behavior.

The most assertive of the women on the staff managed to grab the photo from its not- too -well hidden pile of mail and dance about the office, laughing her head off. The other ladies ran to her and circulated the photo with grabbing gestures. They ended up framing their cheeks between their hands and afterwards placing their hands over their mouths and laughed and laughed.

As luck would have it, the Oracle walked in on the hovering ladies and wanted to know what all the commotion was about. The secretary who had the photo hid it behind her back. Her sleight of hand was of no avail. The superintendent quickly marched into the office circle of clerical workers and grabbed the photo. He turned purple with trembling hands. He had a desire to pee and turned and left as the group of office personnel scattered towards their desks in complete silence.

The superintendent didn't come out of his office prior to everyone calling it a day. But the next day, the superintendent called a meeting of the office staff. He told them that they had acted "unprofessional" and that he had no recourse but to transfer them away from the headquarters office. The secretaries tried to explain, but he silenced them and declared that they had no avenues for explaining their behavior. That was a wrong move because now the office ladies felt wrongfully dismissed to lesser offices.

It was not long before the newspapers received the same photo. However, in a personnel conference with the Superintendent, it was decided that the photo and the possible stories which could be attributed to having posed for the photo, would be outside their purview. The newspapers would not make hay of the story.

The superintendent didn't have a 3"x5" card to tell him what to do. However, he grew more sullen and withdrawn, and soon after, decided to leave the district.

While he wished to be remembered differently, that was not so with the staff members who chose to laugh at the newest way that he would be remembered.

MAKING IT TO EIGHTY

"Dr. Ortiz, you have an urgent call from a Mr. Jay Tollever in San Francisco".

"Doctor, I have good and bad news for you. I have found your grandmother. She's in an elderly residential home in San Francisco, and she has only days to live".

"Oh, my God.......Give me the address, and I'll take the next plane. Send me our total statement for your services and I'll draw up a check when I receive your bill".

As Dr. Mario Ortiz boarded his first class accommodations, he leaned the seat back to relax. He noticed a grandmotherly type lady sitting next to him who seemed self- absorbed in a paperback book. The doctor was tired. The day before he worked long hours with his patients at the office along with performing two complex heart surgeries. When the stewardess saw how quickly he fell asleep, she let him be. The doctor was so fatigued that not even the Captain's voice talking on the speakers aroused him.

After three hours of sleep, he was shaken by the stewardess and the Captain. The lady next to him was slumped in her seat and was not responsive to the smelling salts that were placed in front of her nose. Dr. Ortiz unstrapped her from her chair and had her laid in the aisle and tried to resuscitate her. After giving oxygen and administering CPR, the lady opened her eyes and struggled to take a few deep breaths.

Doctor Ortiz had the lady placed back into her seat. The doctor removed a couple of nitro-glycerin tablets from his black bag and instructed her to place them under her tongue Normally these tablets helped quell fibrillation pulsing of the heart. The doctor recommended that the flight not be re-routed to Reno but should continue to its SFO destination. He asked the Captain to have an ambulance meet the plane.

Dr. Ortiz took advantage of the ambulance ride to Kaiser Hospital. He took a cab to Laguna Honda Hospital and Rehabilitation Center, which was that city's public facility for those in need of care. When he arrived there, he made his way to Dr. Lyon's office since he was the person in charge.

"Yes, Maria Teresa LaFleur is my grandmother. I have been informed by Jay Tollever that she is near death".

"Your grandmother is in a semi-coma. She was in a stable condition until a few days ago. She is not being nourished because she has specified that she is not to be put on any machine or hooked onto any equipment for extending her life."

"I would like to see her".

"I will take you to her".

Maria Teresa was in a room with another woman who probably was awaiting death.

"Dr. Lyons: I need to attempt to talk with her. Let's give her some oxygen and discontinue the pain reducers. I'll stay a few minutes with her".

As ordered by Dr. Ortiz, instructions on the chart were updated to reflect his requests.

The grandson-doctor took a chair next to her and held her hand. He was feeling the pains of guilt. He had not seen his grandmother in years. Yet, he had continued to get her letters and well wishes. Also he knew that she had funded all of his studies. In a soft voice and with tears in his eyes, he said,

"Grandma, I'm here. It's Mario. I'm at your side and if you hear me, wake up because I want to tell you how much I love you".

A nursing assistant came to wheel her bed to another room. Dr. Ortiz followed them to a better-equipped room that had only space for a single bed. The A nurse assistant connected the patient to oxygen and Dr. Ortiz asked them to call the nurse so that Maria Teresa could be placed on intervenes nourishment and medication. Dr. Lyons returned to approve every request that the famous cardiologist requested.

"One more request, doctor", Dr. Ortiz said. "Do you have knowledge of anyone who has been in touch with my grandmother to whom I can direct some non-medical questions? I'd like to know if she expressed herself to anyone. Maybe she had some last thoughts about life or about herself to impart. I'd like to probe that, if it's possible".

Dr. Lyon responded that he thought there might be someone who may be the person that could fill the bill for what the doctor requested. His name is Barnaby Golden, a student from the University. He's in his last year of medical school. He will be getting his degree in psychiatry within the year. Your grandmother has provided us with a written statement because she has volunteered to help the young medical intern. He has been interviewing your grandmother for weeks. Dr. Lyon told Dr. Ortiz that Barnaby Golden had given him his cell phone number. As it turned out, Barnaby Golden was already at Laguna interviewing another patient. He happily agreed to meet with Dr. Ortiz.

As Dr. Lyon withdrew, he had another chair brought into the room so that the pre-med intern and the cardiologist could talk with each other. Barnaby shook hands with Dr. Ortiz and Barnaby expressed himself,

"Doctor, I don't have my notes with me, but I can remember most of everything about Mrs. Ortiz. I had nine sessions with her. I can write a novella about what she and I reviewed about her life. She told me a lot about Hugo, her wonderful husband. She stated that she had a very ordinary life before she met and married him. His parents left him a big house in a suburb of Chicago.

She spent most of her adult life in that wonderful mansion-size house. When they inherited it, the house had little furniture and Hugo told her not to worry. He was a captain of a freighter that made many voyages to Asia. He would see to it that she was able to redecorate their home with what he had already collected in art pieces. He would assure her that many more household goods would be forth coming. In Japan, China, India, Indonesia and the Philippine Islands and Hawaii, he made great purchases with the strong USA dollar. The contents of his huge shipments gave their house a virtual look of a museum.

In Hugo's shipments were many epic Chinese scrolls, Japanese block paintings, Ming dynasty pottery, silk tapestries, fine rosewood furniture, enamel ware, cloisonné, window coverings, and on and on. Hugo wasn't always at her side but, nevertheless, her life was filled with him and his letters, shipments and great times when he returned home.

Maria Teresa had two daughters. They were the greatest children on earth. They were schooled at the best of schools. The auction houses were always willing to purchase items from Mrs. Ortiz. From the sale of all that was surplus or duplicated, money flowed to the LaFleur mansion, allowing them to have the highest level of a living standard.

Your aunt, Flor, married a missionary and traveled with her husband to Tibet. Both she and her husband died in their early fifties from exposure to radiation. I guess they lived too long at a high altitude for them to receive protection from covering layers of air. Both their bodies were returned to Holy Cross Gardens where the LaFleur family had pre-purchased ten grave plots. Flor and her husband were buried next to Hugo who died at seventy-nine, a year before they were interned next to him.

Later your mom, Doña Isabel Ortiz inherited the great house with the remaining furnishings, plus additional sums of money. She never had to work. She lost her husband in the war. Your father never lived to see you because of his pre-mature death in the war.

Your mother and aunt's wealth were the niceties of life which gave them happiness: all provided by Maria Teresa. She sold all her furnishings in her Chicago house. The house itself she gave to Isabel. Maria Teresa moved to the West Coast because Hugo could take an airplane to SFO for the few days it took to load his freighter. When Hugo was in San Francisco, Maria Teresa and Hugo spent quality time until he had to meet his freighter's schedule. In a nutshell, that was her story.

She told me that you were the apple of her eye. She said that she couldn't see how any improvements to her life could ever have been possible. Doctor Ortiz, I feel that I should confess to you that all the old ladies that are living here tell me similar stories to what your grandmother developed for me. It seems that they need to give importance to their lives because they are here and view themselves as impoverished.

It seemed that at times I was not listening because I suspected that what Maria Teresa told me had the characteristics of what others have invented for themselves. On the other hand, I did retain what your grandmother said because there was a more convincing structure to her recollections".

"Barnaby, she was telling you the truth. What I never was told until recently is where our money came from. I won't keep you anymore. You have helped me, and I'll try and understand how she ended up here. I am certain there is a missing piece that I need to latch on to".

The next day, Dr. Ortiz went back to Laguna Honda to pay another visit to his grandmother. He talked to his grandmother. She seemed to be listening to his words. She slowly moved her eyelids and opened her eyes.

"Mario, what are you doing here"?

"Grandmother, why are you here? You know I would have made much better arrangements for your care. I don't understand why you left us without telling us how you were getting along in San Francisco. Grandma, have I ruined these last few years for you by spending all your money"?

"Oh, Mario, you have made me a proud person. You are famous and are doing such wonderful work at your hospital. I'm here because I elected to come here. Hugo had a friend who was cared for and died here. He was a good friend. We didn't have knowledge of his gambling habits that narrowed his options for going forward in greater style. Hugo was so shaken up knowing that his friend died a pauper without ever admitting to his problems. Hugo said that Laguna Honda saved him from the dirt in the streets.

I remember Hugo's gratitude to the staff of Laguna Honda and how it helped his friend during his last days. I'm just an old lady who is also grateful for what life has given me without asking for payback of any kind. Mario, I hope I haven't embarrassed you or your mother. You ought to know that I'm not on the dole because I will take care to reimburse Laguna Honda in a very short while".

"Grandma, I always thought you were rich. Did you spend all your money on my mom and me? I know now that you paid for all of mom's travels and for my total schooling".

"Mario, I'm okay. I really think my money was well spent. Look who you are! I'm the proudest grandmother on planet Earth. Mario, how come I have these machines when I asked to be left alone"?

"Grandma, I needed to have you talk to me. I needed to be wrong about thinking that I was responsible for taking all your money for my expensive schooling. I didn't know that things were not totally right. You know that I love you and will stay here with you".

"I'm glad you woke me up. I can see you as you now are and see my Hugo in you. You must have children and tell them about Hugo and me. Tell them of how great your aunt and her husband were. Tell them that your mother was a great mother and tell them that they, too, are my legacy. Mario, I'll be eighty tomorrow. I hope I can get past midnight so I can be an octogenarian when I die. Mario, what time is it"?

"It's three p.m.".

Maria Teresa slipped into a deep sleep. Mario continued to hold her hand and softly tell her that she would be going back to Chicago with him. Maria Teresa, his grandmother, died after ten p.m. It was after twelve p.m. in Chicago. She lived to be eighty years of age.

Six days later, Maria Teresa's attorney called. Her will was read. Laguna Honda received her donation of $600,000. Museums in Chicago received a million dollars. Should Dr. Mario Ortiz marry, his entire family could travel to Asia and incur no expense. A separate Hugo and Flor fund had been set up for people living at high altitudes to be warned and protected about the damage that can result from the rays of the sun at high altitudes.

Dr. Ortiz received a million dollars. Barnaby received $200,000. Isabel, her middle aged daughter, received $500,000.

"Oh…….Grandma".

MUCH POMP FOR THE CIRCUMSTANCES

"Mitch, when you opened the door, I was not sure you were going to give me a friendly welcome. I know that I should have called to tell you that I needed to see you. Being in the family, I chose not to see you at your office. The problem that I'm having is that I don't know if I have committed a crime. Nevertheless, you have always been honest with me, and your legal experiences allow me to take comfort on whatever advice you may give me.

Mitch, I didn't think I was doing anything wrong when I first broke protocol with the routine of being dined and wined at corporate parties. As you may know, my wonderful butterfly of a wife is in the business of working with many executive types and chief executive officers of notable tech corporations.

Sally and I used to be regulars at their numerous party functions. Dress and etiquette were formal. The conversations at these gatherings were all about the world of technology. It seemed that everything about competitors and start-up companies were of keen interest in the circle of party givers. The more personal information that was introduced, the greater the laughter and back slapping that emanated within the interested huddles that sipped their drinks. In other words, I was hooked to be on that stage, too, because of Sally, who works at Xeromax.

We were in on an exclusive circuit of weekend entertainment. We ourselves hosted a couple of expensive parties at banquet rooms at local restaurants. We didn't use our house for these parties because Sally thought we needed a grander house in order for every one of our groupies to feel comfortable."

"Arne, I haven't seen you or Sally for over ten years. I kept up with both of you by reading the social and business sections of the newspaper. I thought you guys were in a good times whirlwind. You certainly have gone a long way financially since we last met. The newspapers mentioned that through your book sales you are now a millionaire. I see that you now have also been famous for your weekly column in the Sand Times."

"Yes, I have been lucky with my enterprises, but my rise in local fame is now the problem I need to discuss with you. You are an expert on the court system and how it works. That's why I'm here."

"Arne, what have you been up to these last ten years?

I thought you and Sally enjoyed hob-knobbing with the hoi-polloi".

"That was true for eight years. The last two is where I became innovative and came into my own by the turn I made in my thinking".

"Ok, Arne, let's talk. I can't have my only brother stripped of his good reputation or spending time in orange color overalls. We have time to review your suspected problem area because Gussie took the kids to lunch and to see a movie. This gives us time to ponder whatever difficulties that you are having. The coffee is ready. Please fill me in on everything from the beginning. Provide me with as much detail as you can recall".

"Mitch, you understand that keeping neutrality within marriage is difficult, complex, and usually requires a change in behavior and some good acting on our part.

You heard me say that my wife steered us to cocktail parties and that for eight years I hated attending those extraordinary affairs. Sally loves to dress elegantly and go to the hair dresser, the nail salon, and to stores to purchase expensive garments to wear at her corporate get-togethers. I should express to you that I didn't complain. I also liked dressing up. I had my clothes laid out for me. Of course, a note was always left by Sally to remind me that my shoes should be shined, my nails cleaned, and that I should use Brut cologne on myself in order to convey that I belonged with other guys at these stiff-shirt bow-tie gathering.

I should admit that we always tried to arrive late by at least fifteen minutes. At most tech dinner parties, we were re-introduced by the party hostess. The formats for these corporate get-togethers were very similar. Minutes after our arrival, silver trays with hors d'oeuvres took only minutes to be put in front of us. Other trays followed with either champagne or white wine. Crab cakes, or rumaki, were also paraded around the room.

Conversation hummed. Sally usually disappeared into sit-down circles of animated ladies. She left me to seek out acquaintances and strangers who I really was not interested in meeting. However, I made it my business to memorize everyone's name and their title in the corporate world of enterprises. The parties were usually in honor of somebody, some successful venture, or, for some unknown reason other than reciprocity, for earlier gathering of the same people.

Mitch, you must understand that it was impossible to just exist and imbibe the champagne that was delivered in long stemmed fluted glasses. My orders from my spouse were to be much more than the party pooper than I was naturally inclined to be. I had a role to play as Sally's husband. Her demands were for me to stay alert and appear comfortable and talk. After each corporate get together, Sally had me jot down all the persons' names and what they said on 4"x5" cards so that Sally could also take her time to memorize names, rank, and work place.

I usually joined the circle for men who discussed sports, business, managerial corporate strategies and extraordinary gossip. This I did, even though I had little knowledge of products, technology, or stock market quotations. I was definitely an outsider who was infiltrating groups who were in technical career fields. No one cared to probe the altruistic endeavors which comprised my working hours. They just knew I was not part of their industry. They were not interested in who I was. Their hubris for their own business interests was at the core of their exclusive pursuits.

Their labor intensive quests and great ability to focus made them winners in the competitive and innovative fields of new technologies.

Mitch, I must tell you, that while time dragged on for me, Sally was consumed with glee and laughter. She exhibited her refined gestures which included waving her fluted glass contents as if leading an orchestra. She gracefully dipped her strawberries in the chocolate fountain with vibrant shakes of her bejeweled hand. These mini Great Gatsby affairs were very special outings for her. They seemed to energize her for the rest of the week. The women discussed where she bought her long dresses and her exquisite jewelry. For Sally, it was as if St. Peter gave her entry to heaven for week-end social gatherings.

At the Wilson's dinner party, a little crystal bell summoned us to attention in order to give directions to the dining room hidden behind the French louvered doors. We marched in to find the name tags that designated where we were to sit. I usually sat with the most non-interesting nerd or a trophy lady with the kind of wallpaper personality that was used in most designer home bathrooms.

Sally sat next to more important persons. Sometimes, I was aware that she told jokes which I had told her over a period of weeks. However, I thought that was less phony than everything else that was being communicated. The dinner was usually spectacular and wonderfully served. I usually listened with an open ear in order to be able to fill out my 4"x5" cards with detailed information until I arrived home.

When the conversations were outside the realm of technology, great fun was had at the expense of some colorful friends in the trade who cross-dressed, loved dogs more than people, joined nudist camps, had orgies on their yachts, were adroit adulterers, did sky diving, bit their finger nails, fell asleep at board meetings, had Canary Island accounts, etc. After dinner, we broke up individually to tour the house and the gardens. My thought was that housekeepers and gardeners really knew how to get everything appear in magazine-cover shape.

Upon completing the house tour, I latched onto my wife's arm and said that it was time to leave. The neutrality which I spoke about was at an end.

After some whispering in my ear, she simmered down so we could make our excuses for leaving early. As soon as the valet brought the car, I took off my coat, tie, and French cuffs jewelry in order to roll up my starched shirt sleeves and placed everything in the back seat and drove home.

On the way home, my wife said that if I didn't have fun it was because it was my fault. She instructed me not to direct attention to the fact that I was merely a college professor. Gosh! That was somewhat "common place" to such educated, rich persons!

She made me promise that I should behave differently and attempt to find ways to get the attention of important persons in business. Mitch, I told her that I would do that, but she would have to support my ways of meeting her priorities. She wished me to be different and become more interesting at the next party. You have to make them care about "you" for your importance as a college professor.

Eventually, Sally embraced the remarks I made as in so far as promising to be better with what I said, then she became more at ease. After all, she had been complimented and worshipped at the altars of corporate America. I sat down to think of what I needed to do to become important at our next reunions.

The next day, I went to a printer to have business cards made since it was customary to pass them out at these functions to new acquaintances. I felt that I was really unknown to everyone, but I thought that I should play by their rules and make myself known.

Saturday evening arrived; my tux was back from the cleaners, and I was armed with my new business cards that I inserted in a gold case. When we arrived at our destination, the caterers who, as always, dressed in black with white aprons, distributed the appetizers. I joined a huddle of men. I listened carefully to hear strategies and the latest approaches to money laundering and investments.

The hostess of the party, the same woman who provided nothing in conversation when I sat next to her at the last corporate dinner party, welcomed all of us to her home. The hostess' husband was listed in Fortune

500. Everybody, including Sally and I, were greeted as if we were oil persons from Saudi Arabia. It was funny to be treated as an Arab prince since I walked into the party house behind my flamboyant wife.

My wife loved the corsage that had been pinned to her newly purchased elegant gown. The party was not too different from all the others we had frequented, except that no one was passing out their business cards. Since we had arrived late, perhaps I had missed the passing and collecting of the business card ritual.

When Mrs. Wallpaper's helper lady banged a sterling silver spoon on a crystal wine goblet, everyone gave attention. The announcement that she made was that each of us had five minutes to interview the person sitting to the left of us. The purpose of the interview was to have the interviewer give a three-minute oral summary of the person's distinguishing characteristics in their passage to attain business savvy and recognition. Five minutes were spent by my telling the person on the left, my story to gain the group's attention. I had lucked out in my seating arrangement and sat next to a very articulate young woman from Stanford University. She had the task of introducing me to the dinner group.

Most of the introductions were factual, clever, and also interesting. I enjoyed listening to succinct information given about all who were present. I was surprised that the person who introduced my wife knew her entire history and every award and accomplishment bestowed on her.

I introduced the bantam chicken cock of a CEO who sold Mercedes Benz on the internet. My introduction of him was not eloquent but I managed to meet some of his ego needs. He said that he lived up to his advertisements that he made on television. That's why he was in demand. I thought he should have stayed at his agency rather than sit next to me.

Mitch, when the professor from Stanford rose to speak, she surprised the gathering by introducing me as Dr. Goldfink. She related that Dr. Goldfink is a college professor who teaches in the important field of communications. His expertise is delving into the different types of leadership tactics used to achieve high positions at the top rung of an enterprise. He has recently been on sabbatical leave in order to write an insider book on how individual morals are utilized to thrust individuals into positions of power. The premise of the book is that morals and the power that one attributes to oneself contribute to the direction in which the company goes.

This next semester, Dr. Goldfink may be teaching courses on one-upmanship. Much of his research has been gathered at many of the same dinners we are having here tonight. Also, he has a course dealing with making helpful business and social contacts. He said that meetings such as this are very helpful to the exposition of the various innovative business postures that are delineated. Our current business millennium culture is more competitive and cut throat. Therefore, turning the other cheek is a thing of the past in today's business ventures.

He suggests that you take his card if you wish to talk privately with him. He is still revising the text of his book. He invites explicit information from any of you as to how you see yourselves evolve when you achieve more success than you now enjoy. Dr. Goldfink makes certain that all consultations remain confidential and should mention to you that he does not explain his methodology to anyone.

Mitch, you wouldn't believe what happened! There was a strange hush at the table. I saw some of the ladies begin to shiver. Some of them placed their hands over their gaping mouths. At the end of the introductions, we adjourned into a sitting room. All the men also wanted to exit the party.

My wife was in a tizzy. I could tell she was embarrassed. She, too, could not get me out the door fast enough. On the way home, she gave me hell by asking me: how could I do such a thing? How could you say that our friends are going to be cited in your coming book? What are you, a KGB agent? or what? She added that she would never be able to live down her embarrassment. She posed question after question as to what was on my mind.

"Better", she offered, "tell them it's not true. You should have new business cards made advocating that you are a practical joker. Tell them that what you have been writing is not what was said at the dinner table."

My answer was to remind her that she wanted me to have fun at these affairs which needed an injection of realism in our lives. I told Sally that my research for my book or books was contained in all of the 4"x5" cards that she made me document for eight years. In fact, I said to Sally that I predict that if there are future parties, the party givers will be seating us with more selectivity. My books were well received, and I, too, made money. However, I also have several law suits pending because of some denials to what I have written.

On the other hand, Sally continues to be amazed that I have received notoriety. We continue to be invited to many parties. The number of companies entertaining us are now quite diverse. I am in demand as a college professor and author. In the last two years, I have published several money-making books.

Do you know the best thing of all? Now, I'm dragging Sally to parties that at times she is unsure she wishes to attend. I think that now she would rather go to her yoga classes than to parties".

"That is some story, Arne. I guess Sally is no longer in hiding from her corporate friends.

Let me tell you how I think this will come out. Some people may claim that you are a scoundrel. That may be true. However, that's not illegal or bad. I gather that you are being sued by executives who have become public persons. Once that kind of fame is established, they cannot shield themselves from publicity.

You are safe from being sued if you have your dated 4"x5" cards which detail each get-together and also prove authenticity insofar as written comments and theories. No, I don't see that you have done anything that can be constituted as a criminal act.

Unknowingly, Sally and you now share the same social rung as Gussie and I. Sally probably wouldn't hold it against me that I am a bail bondsman and that I have to associate with some shady characters. We can now plan to see each other on a more frequent basis.

Brother, we are both scoundrels and our wives will adjust to our new behaviors and endeavors. After all, they still shop for what they see and buy new to replace old. I'm certain they don't really feel deprived of anything. Please send me copies of your books. I'd love to read them.

So, cheers! Let us now click our coffee mugs and cheer our getting together after ten years"!

I THOUGHT I WAS RETIRED

After the inscribed gold watch was awarded him for his thirty-six years of service, Somerset Hughes climbed aboard his large size, well designed recreational vehicle and headed north to his brother's ranch.

Somerset's pre-packed treasures consisted of favorite books that he wished to re-read; a professional camera; fishing poles, and a shotgun. Attila, his black Labrador, was always ready to join Somerset in the front passenger seat. His planned escape to forego the life he feared could materialize if he remained in town in search of things to do. Therefore, he took to the road with no set date for his return home.

He steered his RV towards his brother's ranch. It was located in a meadow between mountains within the Trinity Mountain Range. His was not a long drive and he completed his journey in total daylight. Upon his arrival, he was greeted by Elena, his brother's wife, and Bandido, a much larger, huskier, black Labrador than Attila. His brother and their 15-year old son, Jody, were away at their nearby Hughes Wilderness Camp for families who wished to learn survival skills and rough it for a week or two.

As the skies darkened, Somerset watched Elena prepare supper. After drinking his can of beer to the half-way mark, the rest of the family came in to joyously greet and welcome him. As always, the dogs remained outside. The Labs had been acquainted with each other during other stays in which the brothers got together at the ranch. After they parked Somerset's RV about a football field distance from the house, he told his brother that he planned to be self-sufficient and use his RV as a summer home. He needed to read books, to fish and hike on the nearby fire trails that were maintained by the fire department of the Department of Forestry.

Elena extended him an open invitation to come to supper or sleep over at any time he needed their company or the warmth of their home. Jody loved to talk with his uncle. He was an intelligent youth who attended a prestigious academy in Oregon that combined the caring of livestock with a strong academic program emphasizing methodological and investigatory research skills. On the day that followed the arrival of Somerset to the pastoral spot, Jody decided to remain at home instead of going off with his dad to help out at the Hughes Wilderness Camp.

Jody had no qualms about going to his uncle's RV and banging on his door. Jody wanted to talk. He told his uncle all about what he was learning at school. Somerset listened carefully. He asked if he was happy in learning what was being taught at his school.

"Yes, and no" Jody answered. "I think that our government class is too superficial because it falls short on details and contextual contents. Uncle, what do you suppose thinking is"?

"That's a great question. The way I see it is concentration and thinking about what is up front in your mind. It takes looking at what you want to explore. At times it takes tenacity and courage to stand apart from those who hold thoughts which are prejudicial and locked onto ideological presumptions. Looking at a perceived problem or idea in a critical manner doesn't mean holding fast to what others think. This means looking into the pros and cons that exist. Then evaluating each factor specifically in order to distill a statement or question to its bare roots.

Make certain that you are not allowing yourself to lean in a particular direction prior to concluding your probe. In other words, it's not good enough to accept thinking that the world is or isn't round if you wish to be precise and accurate.

You are in school to learn math and science so that you can be clear on what you believe is true fact. You want to communicate transparent thoughts to others who seek accuracy and wish to add to their knowledge. Most persons will have scientific agreement that the world is sphere-shaped. You can agree that this is so because it's been proven in research. Store what you learn and know that there will be denial of any fact you hold to be true by a segment of the population who thrives on repeating that which was last told or heard by them. Be careful on accepting that which is told by persons who you know have a set agenda.

The kind of thinking I'm suggesting you follow is sometimes a very lonely road to travel. Society likes to run on what is provided them by traditional ideology, dogma, rules of behavior, and whims. Putting unique thinking into vocal or written words sometimes results in losing friends, being made fun of, and possibly stirring up an anonymous army against your expressed thoughts".

Just then, Jody's cell phone rang and his mom told him lunch was ready.

"Uncle, can I come back and have you tell me more"?

"Yes, but in the meantime, think of why your class in government is not totally satisfying your appetite for learning. If you have time, you might want to read about the thoughts of the Dutch philosopher Spinoza. Here is a book summarizing his ideas".

It was decided that Jody and his uncle would get together the next morning. Somerset and Attila hiked the nearby trails that afternoon. The next morning, Jody was revved up and asked many questions about thinking and probing and how it is that we learn. He made reference to Spinoza and told his uncle he understood the reason that he was told that it was just another way of looking at the subject of thinking. They talked about animal thinking and particularly about the ways primates learn to solve basic survival problems. Somerset asked what Jody found lacking in the subject he studied in his government class.

"Uncle, the teacher read us the Declaration of Independence but left it to us to absorb the meaning of the words. I did understand why the Declaration of Independence said "all men are created equal". We wanted ourselves free from what England had imposed on the colonists. However, I don't understand it. Why does that kind of language appear there when it never was inserted into the U.S. Constitution"?

"Jody, equality is an ideal that we need to hope for but may never realize. There are probably immature men who always like to label others as inferior to themselves. No matter where you are on the social strata, there are persons who artfully create social and economic rungs below the one they believe they stand upon. Equality is the best of all possible worlds, and, seemingly, we lost the optimum opportunity to establish equality years ago.

We know that equality can, at times, be more than an ideal. It can become a principle or basic truth for small gatherings of people. Equality could have existed in the days of pioneers when agricultural-minded farmers who traveled together to find new lands. They had to rely on each other to achieve their mission and for remaining safe. Equality demands stepping down from self-given and unmerited self-esteem. Some men need to bestow that kind of aura on themselves. Imaginary class-separating hierarchies and self-denial are problems that can be eradicated in an emergency when there is adherence to a common cause greater than self-postulation.

For example, a sinking ship which has the crew take to lifeboats changed the concept for equity because all are equal to share the same lifeboat in order to survive. Once safely off the lifeboat, the equality status once employed doesn't usually last. Education is sometimes a rationed commodity for those who theoretically are emancipated or who only recently walk inside our national boundaries. Of all the ideals that are known to us, freedom and equality are of the highest order.

Nevertheless, in some communities man still lives by his Neanderthal ways of dealing with persons from different tribes. Today, men can purchase guns to rescue themselves in case the situation ever presents itself to retain the upper hand. Generally, relying on a weapon to be the equalizer gives some people the excuse against who are those thought not to be their equal. The real problem we all share is that we are here on earth for a very brief time. Everyone should make the most of the time we have. The three amendments that were added to the original U.S. Constitution ruled that "equal" should exist as a right in local state and federal elections.

Equality is worth pursuing. It's not easy to do so, but it helps to make the most by living with the belief that we must continue to work towards achieving equity. We are in trouble when we view each other as being in separate life boats and are not connected to one another".

During Somerset's afternoon walks with Attila, he reviewed his morning talks with his likable nephew. Indeed Jody was a great kid. His keen mind sponged up what was discussed. His refined questions were becoming a methodology, possibly paradigms. Somerset, himself, was having a great time. He loved learners. And he loved his place in the outdoors as much as Attila rejoiced over his new environment.

The expected knock on the door was accompanied by Jody who had shinning eyes on his alert face. He was there to talk. That was his phraseology of what his uncle and he were doing during their morning times. After a review of yesterday's talk, Jody asked if liberty and freedom were the same. According to his dictionary, he couldn't gauge any difference. Somerset had to think if there was a distinction between either in the quality of life. He indicated that maybe "liberty" implied a governmental structure and "freedom" was more apt to be an individual state of being.

The morning sessions ended when Elena, Sebastian, and Somerset took Jody to the train station so that he could return to Oregon to begin the new school quarter. Before boarding the train, Jody was given Somerset's cell phone number. Jody wrote it down on his note book and promised to call everyone once a week.

When the rains came down hard, Sebastian and Somerset closed up the Hughes Wilderness Camp and began to work together. Somerset was always invited to have supper at his brother's home. One evening, when Somerset was back in his RV and had finished re-reading "Don Quijote", his cell phone rang. It was Jody.

"Uncle, my civics teacher gave me a "C", the lowest grade she gives, because I did what you said was good to do when there was need to express myself accurately. She said that President Lincoln freed the slaves. I wrote that while he did set the stage that helped pass laws that led to three constitutional amendments and gave African Americans their freedom, he did it in harmony with the concepts included because the Declaration of Independence was the premise for bonding this nation. I questioned why it took three amendments of the Constitution - very late in time from 1776 - to spell out what the founders of the country had already agreed to and stipulated in the splendidly worded Declaration of Independence.

I also wrote that "self-evident" had not yet been achieved. We were all created equal as a political ideal or promise. The economics of the southern states thought that enterprises trump our political ideals and also the laws fostering equality and freedom for slave African Americans."

"Jody, I'm sorry you got the "C", but I am proud of what you wrote in your essay. Now you begin to see how your individual thinking sometimes falls on locked brains. Your teacher is not a marble head, but she needs to understand from you your thinking about what you have read and discussed. You and the teacher should have a talk in the way you and I had this summer. Ask for time to explain your thoughts to her. If she gets defensive, then know that you have to suffer the course in loneliness but you'll maintain and gain in your manhood".

"Thanks, Uncle. I'll do just what you say. Don't tell Dad about my bad grade yet. Perhaps Ms. Sullivan will see my logic in what I wrote in my essay. I loved what I wrote in my essay. Thanks, Uncle".

Four evenings after Jody had called his Uncle, he called. Somerset knew it was Jody before putting down his book "Travels with a Donkey" and gave his nephew his big "hello".

"Uncle, I spoke to Ms. Sullivan. I explained that I took good notes on what she told us in class. I also told her that I read excerpts of several history books on the subject of equality. I explained my point of view to her. She asked me to tell her what the source was that helped form my conclusions. I replied that I was the source of my thoughts. She laughed. She told me that now she better understood me and my explanation of thoughts as written in my essay.

Again, she laughed. Uncle, it was a good-natured laugh. She asked me if I felt that I deserved an "A". I answered that my thoughts were to learn and think clearly about how to see things. I think she was a little surprised at how serious I was about my studies. Then, she replied,

'Jody, you are too much. Go on…..get out of here'.

Uncle, what do you think? Will she upgrade my" C" grade"?

"Jody, I think you did yourself good. Your teacher may have changed your grade. What's important is that she knows you take pride in what you do. I know that in future essays she will take care in reading your approach to your self-expression of what you have studied.

Keep up your ways of pursuing thinking. Nephew, I'm proud of you"!

Now that Jody was away and his brother had closed the camp, Sebastian would help his brother enlarge his house and assist Elena with the household chores.

Hopefully, he and his brother would have time to hunt and fish. When it rains, Somerset would re-read all the books that he had for such a happening. Great reads would certainly keep his mind engaged doing what he loved.

THE CRUISE

Miss Abigail Katuna always had taken pride in the fact that she had remained a virgin all her life. She was now in her late sixties or early seventies and took pride in the virtuous life she was able to live.

Her claim of being a proud, celibate person was designated by wearing a long white scarf around her shoulders on a daily basis throughout her lifetime. When she taught high school, all her students were made aware of her eccentricity. This consisted in verbally stating who she was and representing her symbolic purity by wearing her clean white scarf. No one had to encourage Miss Abigail (as she was called) to defend her moral code or her sometimes verbally expressed female status of never having slept in the same bed with another person. Maybe she held a record for being who she actually was: a celibate lady.

Aside from the public image she perpetuated, Miss Abigail was seemingly well adjusted in her total persona. She had a number of women friends who respected her for her knowledge of literature and history. She was also fun when she puffed herself up discussing kinky passages occurring in literature or history. Her wonderful vocabulary reigned when she was forced to render an opinion reflecting her disdain of promiscuous passages contained in classical literature or historical lore in the escapades of the powerful. She thought the "Canterbury Tales" were on a par with the essays of the Marquis de Sade.

Miss Abigail was usually invited to baby showers, anniversary celebrations, bridge parties, marriages, etc. Hostesses always alerted those who were not acquainted with her to steer away from references to any sexual encounters. Jokes about sex which didn't have redeeming aspects were also placed on the taboo list when Miss Abigail was present.

One day, Miss Abigail was reading the obituary page and recognized the name of Cyrus Hallahan. He was the husband of Nellie Hallahan, a teacher-friend of Miss Abigail. Miss Abigail decided to attend the memorial service for him since she really liked Nellie. Attending the service, Miss Abigail hugged her friend Nellie, and they exchanged personal information in order to meet at a future time.

Four months later, Nellie called Miss Abigail in order to invite her to a High Tea that was being promoted in a neighborhood tea garden. The two retired women met and enjoyed each other's company. Nellie opened her bag and unfolded a commercial announcement for a 12-day voyage for "two at the price of one" on the top deck of a new cruise ship going from San Francisco to five Hawaiian Islands. Miss Abigail became interested when she focused on the fact that there were suites with twin beds. Why not? That kind of adventure was something to look forward and to escape the obituary notices of people who were in their age bracket.

Once aboard the massive cruise ship, it seemed that the adventure was going to be great: movies, entertainment, eats of all kind, games, a library, and deck chairs. However, Murphy's Law kicked in on the third day. Nellie reported that she didn't feel well. Abigail summoned the ship's doctor. He shook his head and asked Nellie if she had been around young children. Nellie replied that prior to her going on the cruise, she had spent the day with three of her grandchildren.

"Well, Miss Hallahan, you have the measles and that means that you and Ms. Katuna will have to be quarantined. You will not be able to leave your cabin. We will provide all your meals and beverages and any service which either of you require. You'll have to stay in your cabin until I allow you to leave. This is for your protection and the protection of all other passengers.

You will not be charged for this trip. On de-boarding, you will get full reimbursement. I'm very sorry about this medical situation. However, by following my instructions and taking the medication that I'll send up to you, you will recover fully. Hopefully, Miss Katuna, you have had the measles before and will not be subjected to catching them again. However, you are not to leave this cabin".

Nellie felt awful in that she had spoiled the trip for Abigail. Basically, they were prisoners in their wonderful cabin and could only view the vast ocean through portholes. With everything going wrong, Miss Abigail continued to cover her shoulders with one of her white scarves.

Nellie was a more outward-going person because she had taught science and physical education classes in her career at the same high school that Miss Abigail taught government and history classes. Nellie knew all about Miss Abigail's symbolic white scarf and set that quirk aside as an idiosyncrasy which did not detract negatively when weighed against Miss Abigail's total attributes.

"Abigail, I'm so sorry I brought on this situation. Now we are stuck, and I guess we'll be reading a lot of books. I must admit that you seem to be taking this catastrophe amicably".

"Nellie, My philosophy is that age has the advantages that allows the unexpected to be expected. We are not often in control of what happens around us".

"May I call you 'Abby' now that we are existing as sisters?"

"Why, yes, that name was last used when I was a teenager."

"Abby, I know who you are, and I very much respect you. You really don't have to wear your scarves unless someone knocks on our door to bring us something".

"Nellie, my problem is that by now I feel naked when I'm not carrying the scarf".

"Abby, I understand that. As I lay here, I hope that I will not die. Curiously, I'm wrapped in memories of my long life. I'd like to tell you about what I am thinking now so that my memories can be visualized by an understanding person. May I do that"?

"Nellie, dear, you're not going to die. Death doesn't sneak up on us old ladies. It usually comes around when we are not ailing or worried about situations which block us from family or friends. I'd be glad to hear whatever you have riding in your mind about yesterday's occurrences".

"Abby, I had a boyfriend before I met Cyrus. My first beau was Ido, a handsome devil, who was new to the United States. He was from Yugoslavia. He was so amorous. He always brought me a single rose in a flower flask. He had an old car, and we went way out in the country. One day while on a lonely mountain trail, he kissed me so that I felt his sexual energy all the way to my toes. I kissed him back and eventually passion took over us on the grassy hillside. The world spun and we perspired together for a long time.

I took that as a high point in my young life and as a unification that we would marry. That could have been, except that Ido was killed two days later when he was on a six-car pileup on a busy highway. All I materially had from Ido was a bunch of empty flower flasks to indicate that we had found love.

In my memory, his love has never been replaced. None of my dates steamed me to the state that I was in on that long ago mountain pasture. That feeling has never left me in life. I could tell you more but if I do, I will cry. I have just told you what I haven't told anyone. Cyrus had no idea that Ido still exists within me.

My second and third beaus were nice kids. We did a lot of kissing and touching, but we never had intercourse. By then I had the fear that friendships were temporary and not worthy of the consequences of experimenting and in calling up fervent hormones into play. It was in college that I met my Cyrus. He was already balding, but he also had great blue eyes and wonderful black eyebrows. Best of all, he was intelligent and could sing many folk ballads. As you know, he became an architect. As soon as he found employment in his field, he came to the house, gave me a big hug and lifted me in his arms and sung to me. He gave me his ring, and we married three months before I received my teacher's credential.

For two years we traveled in the USA, Canada, Ireland, and most of Europe. Cyrus was in demand. He saw what was not there in other buildings. He put the missing parts there, and he was much applauded with publicity, contracts, and had the admiration of his colleagues. After six children and now eleven grandchildren and one great grandchild, my memories are embedded joyously in births, birthdays, holidays, outings and, of course, with some agony when recalling funerals and a divorce or two. Abby, I have as many memories as I have secrets. I'm talking too much without giving you the opportunity to say something about yourself".

"Nellie, I don't have memories of any boys that I have liked. When I was a senior in high school, one young man who bought me a hamburger and milkshake asked me if I would show him me. I slapped him silly and walked home from that drive-in where we were.

Once on a trip to Spain, my sister and I were approached by an official guide. We didn't understand what he was saying, but when we looked at our English-Spanish dictionary, it seemed that he wanted to give us a bath. We yelled at him to have him understand that we didn't need to be bathed by him. A bystander later explained that he wanted to show us the Roman Baths. So you see, Nellie, life hasn't had the embellishments that you have experienced. I have never been loved by persons outside my family, nor have I been emotionally hurt. I was not made to be anything other than a spinster.

On the other hand, my sister was not like me. She went to a nude beach in Spain. When she described in detail what she saw, my curiosity of how Homo sapiens can prance about when they have no restrictions is appalling. I could never have taught science as you did. I once saw a film on how elephants mate. The three-foot erect curved penis of the bull was so horrifying to me that I immediately made my excuse from the National Geographic lecture on endangered wild animals. That visualization was almost nightmarish to me".

The ship's doctor paid his daily visit and informed Nellie that if she wished, she could be hospitalized on Oahu for a couple of days and then fly home. However, we decided that we would remain on board ship until Nellie's bout with the measles was over. In looking back over the last few days, our confinement to quarters was not the hardship that it could have been if we hadn't gotten along so well.

Abigail, particularly, had enjoyed the fact that Nellie had taken her into her confidence. She decided to tell Nellie what she had been hiding for over fifty years.

"Nellie, I want to tell you about what has lead to the mistrust of others. Is that okay with you? It's the kind of confidence you shared with me about your love for Ido.

I come from a dysfunctional family. My mother married young. She was very good looking and my father was not. He was more like Attila the Hun. They dated for about a year when he married mother. I don't know why my mother married him, since she must have had other men from this country interested in her. None-the-less, she married father to suffer from his phobic ways.

He was a house painter and drank his fill at every opportunity that a bottle of booze was handy. He was extremely jealous and didn't permit my mom to leave the house without him. He became sort of maniacal in that he painted all the windows that faced the street, black. When he left for work, he would also lock up all my mother's dresses so that she couldn't leave the house. On cold days, mom had to cover herself with blankets. We had no telephone and only listened to the outside world on the radio.

My mother cried a lot. She and I cried together. My sister was four years younger than I was and didn't understand our situation. Somehow, Social Services came to the house but we could not let them in. My mom talked to the Social Service worker though the closed front door. She told her that she had children ages two and six and did not have a dress on. That same evening, the social workers came at six o'clock and my father answered the front door. Mom was still in her underwear. The house was a mess.

Trouble was in the making. My tough-guy father was eventually deported because he was wanted for some crime in his country. Mom was too frail to take care of us, so we were placed in foster homes. My sister and I were lucky to have been placed with a wonderful woman who was married to a traveling FBI agent. Nellie, tell me, do you think I'm silly with my adherence to thinking I'm someone special because I have led a virtuous life"?

"If honesty doesn't shake our friendship, I'll tell you what I think. I'll skip that which deals with the wonderful person that you are and dwell on what I think you are referencing. Your scarves are a shield and guard you from meeting and getting to know other persons. In my mind, that's not a positive. I recall Mr. Andrews, our other science teacher, was very interested in having a date with you. He asked his friends on the faculty what they thought about his asking you for a date. I must have told him what others had already said. I said 'don't bother Ms. Hallahan as she is untouchable and will not understand the reason for your interest in her.'

Abby, measles have been a wonderful experience for me because of you. You are special, scarf or no scarf. You have limited the kinds of joys that life usually gives you to take. That's it. Are we still friends"?

Abigail cried and hiccupped her crying "thank you" to Nellie.

Three days later, the measles subsided and the two friends joined the activities aboard ship. When they docked in San Francisco, both ladies made their way to take a cab. Nellie turned to Abby and said,

"Abby, you forgot your scarf"!

"No, Nellie....... I don't need it"!

A STEP IN RAISING HERBIE

Persons who watch Eduardo Lopez' crushed legs bend awkwardly as he walked had to have the idea that he wouldn't get too far before he leaned too far to one side or the other and fell.

Six years prior, Eduardo and his painter partner fell from a five-story building when their scaffold hooks snapped and plunged them to the sidewalk. Eduardo survived the fall, but his friend who had teamed with him on big painting projects did not. His fall crippled his legs and blunted his once active life. The girl he was engaged to at the time of his accident left him. She knew that the $350,000 he received from the building's insurance company would not sustain him for his expected lifetime and would constrict him from having a meaningful future.

Eduardo had to use crutches to assist his traveling on the city sidewalks. He understood his serious predicament and decided to go outdoors only to take care of his clothing and nourishment needs. Most of the time, his next door neighbor with his thirteen and eleven year-old boys would help him by doing his errands to attain some of his daily needs.

His neighbor, Pascual, the father of the boys who assisted him, was a great friend. He taught Eduardo to play the guitar and how to pluck the notes of the chords written on sheet music. Eduardo counted on Pascual sending his limit of one beer per evening since neither wished Eduardo to regress to the drinking habit he once had as a busy house painter.

Pascual's two boys liked Eduardo. He was funny and could recall all that he heard on his radio into humorous stories when politicians offered inane solution to solve complex problems that they wished to solve with talk. He mimicked them as ignoramuses on the loose. The nuttiness reported on the radio was also made into funny situations by Eduardo. Pascual's children were good company to Eduardo, and he missed their visitations on nights when they had substantial homework.

Eduardo's sister, Marina, lived two hundred miles in another city. She was a single mom and had a twelve year old boy named Herbie. When Marina contracted lymphatic cancer, she called Eduardo and told him of the probable narrow odds she had for recovery. Outside of Herbie, Eduardo was the only family she had to ask for help in caring for Herbie.

Eduardo confided this situation and personal dilemma to his friend Pascual. At an earlier time, it had been his hope that if his sister decided not to get married that he and she could share living quarters to ease one another's financial burdens. Instead, now he was going to have to be his nephew's guardian – a youngster who he had no idea how to take care of him. Pascual said,

"Don't worry. Your sister's condition is our primary concern. We have to help her. Let's tell her we will be at her place this Saturday to pick up Herbie along with all his belongings. We'll rent a van and transport him back to your place".

Arriving at her place on Saturday morning was fortunate for Herbie because the ambulance was also there to transport Marina to the hospital. Eduardo just had time to hold her hand and obtain all the papers which transferred legal custody of his nephew to him. Giovanni and Paulo helped Herbie settle down by allowing him to talk out his swirling vortex of miseries.

No more than ten days had past and things were beginning to be situated insofar as getting Herbie registered at school and making Eduardo's place suitable to house him, when bad news arrived. Marina had died. She had been cremated. As she wished, her ashes were disposed by the mortuary. She now only existed with Eduardo and Herbie in their memories.

Once the mental shock and after-thoughts were in remission, Herbie also began to appreciate the Uncle he previously had not known well. He embraced the companionship provided by the boys who lived on the same floor next door. The doors to each apartment were left open when there was back and forth movement between the extended family friends.

As soon as Pascual was home from working at the city's produce market, Eduardo had him come over to carry whatever he had made for dinner to Pascual's house. He wanted to demonstrate his appreciation for helping him raise Herbie. He also loved it when both families ate their dinners together.

When Eduardo was alone with Pascual, he expressed his inadequacies in answering Herbie's questions concerning sex. He once had a fiancé who always told him, "no, no, no" until we're married. He was not clear about how to explain things about which he himself was not totally certain. Pascual acknowledged that boys obtaining information about sex would be a piecemeal process which would probably be demeaning to the opposite sex. In order to prevent that from happening, he thought that he better sit down and have a talk with all of them. Since the produce market was closed on Saturdays, it was a good time to gather everyone.

"Boys, you are of that baffling age when your bodies are making or about to make an enormous transition, and you need to begin to understand how wonderful nature is to all of us. The next few years will be the start for nature to work its bodily changes. These changes are normal and occur in all healthy boys. Usually girls your same age have their growth spurt sooner and quicker.

The changes of which I speak also affect and are making transitional changes in your sexual organs. This will be a time to be confident and happy about what is happening because eventually you will become adult men. The girls will become young ladies. What everyone hopes is that boys who become men will also learn to be gentlemen. To be a gentlemen starts about the ages that you are at now.

Girls also need special practice in attainment to receive special treatment by boys. They will blossom with the help of being treated and thought of as receiving compliments from polite boys. For example, boys have to take precaution not to hurt a girl's feelings. It's also okay to make a girl feel good by telling her she is special in personality, looks, intelligence, or in the way she talks, walks, sits, and asks a boy to do friendly things like walking beside her or carrying things for her. If a girl asks you a question because she likes you, make sure you pay her attention. If she asks if you think she is pretty, you must tell her "yes". "Yes" does not hurt her feelings. A "yes" answer is always okay to give concerning questions about her looks, hair, dress, and behavior.

Sometimes there are contrary and demeaning thoughts made about girls by silly boys who don't know how to act in the presence of girls. They will make fun of a girl's breast size, pimples on her face, about the way she arranges her hair, or by suggesting that she is a bad or nasty person because of malicious hear-say.

Such behavior is not a worthy way for gentlemen to behave. Don't you guys fall into such a conversational trap! Never take the bait of what a boy says to demean a girl. Every girls, skinny or fat, tall or short, is the person who has much to give in friendships. Remember that most girls can someday be mothers. How special is that?

You boys know you once had that very special person in our lives. You never gain respect for your behavior by departing from the values we hope you will always demonstrate. When you acquire more learning and skills, you'll want to be honest and loyal to us, your parents. You do know that we should always be truthful with one another. We are a cheerful, fun-loving - and at the same time – serious members of families that want to be the best that they can be".

Herbie felt that the mysterious body changes Pascual mentioned were difficult to comprehend. His mother never lifted the curtain to the subject of changes in the body that were being surfaced at the kitchen table.

"Pascual, will I have crooked legs like my uncle when my body changes"?

Everybody laughed. Pascual brought seriousness back into play and said,

"No, you will start to get more muscle, probably more hair throughout your body and the size of your penis will grow. It changes because you will have testicles and a larger sack behind your penis. Haven't you seen adult men"?

"No. Can you show me yours"?

"No, but I can sketch an adult penis for you after we talk. Don't be in a hurry to deal with your curiosity. Everything will happen in good time".

Herbie said,

"But, Pascual, I don't even like girls. My mother confused me when she made me promise that I would marry a very nice girl and have many children. She wanted me to make sure if I had a daughter, I would name her after her. Will I get to like girls in the future"?

"Oh, Herbie, your mother was just encouraging you to be a great man with high ideals. You do not have a problem. Many years from now, you will incur a special magnet to new feelings for a special young lady. From then on, things will happen and maybe your mother's wishes for you will be set into motion. You can respectfully tell that nice girl that she has made your little bell inside alerting you to need her very special friendship. She will understand because you may also have her head ringing with happiness. It may be that soon after you will want to buy her a ring".

"Pascual, not all girls are nice".

"The nice ones will get nicer with time. The ones that are not wonderful to you may change when you continue to be polite and respectful to them. Remember what I said that young girls need practice in being in the company of boys and sometimes they act silly because they are getting their own feelings organized. No more questions.

I think that what we should do this afternoon is to go to the museum. There you will see how proud we are of our bodies. Great artists have depicted their love of religious rites and the way they wished to capture beauty to canvas".

The museum tour proved to be an eye opener. Beautiful masterpieces displayed the different world and those which captured life as they saw it. The years went by. Eduardo began to master playing his guitar. To his surprise, Herbie had a wonderful voice. The two of them could entertain new neighbors and friends. They were in demand at small parties and receptions.

Eduardo often thought to himself: "Pascual helped me but I also am doing a great job raising my nephew. I'm one lucky guy to live where I live and have the family that I have".

By the time Giovanni, Herbie, and Paolo were in high school, they became very popular with their singing while Eduardo expertly strummed his guitar. At high school, the girls became so friendly that they all wanted to be in the company of such popular boys.

Pascual was always present to insure that all of the family be taken home in his new SUV. Herbie told Eduardo and Pascual that he really liked a beautiful brunette who followed the singing group wherever they played.

Pascual said, "Keep an eye on her because she is a very ingratiating person. She is worth having as a friend.

However, remember that college is next. Giovanni loves college and wants you to join him".

I'M NOT HIM

Today was the first day of the December Holiday Season at the San Francisco Public Schools, and the schools are not in operation. Teacher Steve Higgins planned his day so he could visit the Legion of Honor Museum. He wanted to see the visiting exhibition of Dutch and Flemish painters before it left to another renowned museum.

Steve purposely arrived there with time to see the familiar sculptors which surround the wonderful museum. When he went up to get a close-up of the massive statue of El Cid upon his prancing horse, he heard the clicking of a camera. He turned around and saw that a guy about his age who was clicking away at him standing in front of El Cid, the great Spanish warrior-politician who unified Spain and successfully emancipated his country from Moorish domination.

"I hope you don't mind my taking photos of you with El Cid in the background. For some reason, you look familiar to me. Allow me to introduce myself, I'm Henry Lightfoot"

Steve was suspicious of this guy in that he was overly friendly in his introduction and the fact that he had taken so many photographs of him.

Steve Higgins said, "My name is Steve. Please excuse me, but the museum is now opening its doors and I have to run so that I can beat the crowds that will begin to form at any time".

As always, the visiting exhibition was wonderful to view. On leaving the Legion of Honor, Steve headed for his car that was parked near the spectacular statue of Joan of Arc. Before he reached his car, the same Henry Lightfoot came up to him and asked,

"Aren't you Simon Peters?"

"Sorry, you have the wrong guy".

"Listen, Simon, we were once great buddies. If you have something to hide it's safe with me. Can we get a beer and discuss the great time we had when we were together on R and R in Osaka and Kyoto, Japan"?

"I don't mean to be impolite, but I am not the person you are naming Simon Peters. Anyway, you have a great day for yourself. Goodbye".

"Before you go, here is my name and phone number in case you ever want to talk about our time together in Japan".

Steve took the paper that was handed to him, closed the car door and left. As Steve Higgins sat at home having a cup of coffee and peanut butter on toast, his mind returned to what Henry Lightfoot implied. He sensed that he had heard Lightfoot's name and voice before. Lightfoot's voice was familiar, although he didn't recall meeting him prior to today. He realized that he had been impolite to Lightfoot. Maybe the old guy deserved a less hurried response than the abruptness he had exhibited towards him.

Steve found Lightfoot's paper which had his telephone number and called it. Once both were on the telephone, Steve invited Lightfoot to the International Pancake House on Saturday morning. On Saturday morning, the two of them sat in a back corner of the restaurant to converse in a quiet booth that was away from the main body of folks in the restaurant.

"Tell me why you think you know me" asked Steve?

Lightfoot opened an album he carried and said,

"Tell me if this is you. Listen, if you are now in the CIA or are in a Witness Protection program, know that you can remain Steve, and I'll never again allude to you as Simon Peters. You'll just have to trust me. Look at these photos".

Lightfoot had a page and a half of photos in his album. The photos showed Steve and Hank Lightfoot in Marine uniforms with a bevy of Japanese girls seemingly escorting them around the outstanding landmarks of their beautiful city. Steve's hand trembled. He didn't remember Henry Lightfoot or being with him in Japan.

"Honestly, Hank, I don't remember any of this. I can't explain this at all"!

"Wait, Steve, there's more. You were reported as missing in action. From the time of the accident, it's been over seven years before the Marine Corps designated you as a casualty of the Korean War".

"What were you and I doing in Japan"?

"We were on Rest and Recreation. We were from different outfits and met at the Corps base located in the Osaka-Nagoya area. These ladies in the photos all had green cards and updated medical approval to escort servicemen. Steve, we had a great week. We were taken in a chauffeured limousine to a very nice hotel. That's where we later met Nabuko and Yoshima. On my second R&R when you were not with me, I went out with Nabuko on a fulltime basis. We're still together because we married in 1960".

"Hank, I don't remember anything. What's wrong with me"?

"How does your discharge list you"?

"My Honorable Discharge states that I am Sergeant Steven Higgins. Hank, I'm not lying to you. I don't recall any of what you are telling me. I believe you because your voice sounds very familiar to me. Who is this other Japanese lady that I have my arms around in the photo".

"That's Yoshima, the lady you thought that you wanted to marry. For your information, Yoshima still writes to Nabuko. She has never married but is a very rich lady because her father left her his hotels. We've gone back to see her four times. Her generosity is a forever quality that characterizes her. Steve, Yoshima knows the details of your death because her father had the accident you were in investigated. That's all that I know. If you want to come to our house, Nabuko may be able to tell you more".

On Sunday, Steve went to Lightfoot's house. He met Nabuko, and her voice also sounded very familiar. She was a very petite good looking grey-haired lady. After they talked, Steve requested Nabuko to call Yoshima but not to mention why she was being asked about Steve Higgins.

The telephone call was made to Kyoto and Steve heard another voice that he seemed to recognize coming through on the speaker phone. After a few moments of silence, Yoshima read from a Japanese newspaper an article which announced the deaths of six marines and two American politicians. A cargo/transport plane in route from Japan to Oahu crashed into the Pacific Ocean.

Only two survivors were found floating on a wooden bench. One of the survivors was Marine Corps Sergeant Steven Higgins from Pomona, California. Sergeant Higgins was taken to Tripler Hospital in Oahu in critical condition. The other survivor of that mysterious crash was Sergeant Alonzo Anderson. He was also taken to Tripler Hospital and was lucid for a while, but never recovered from his severe internal injuries. He died three weeks later. The rest of the other personnel's bodies in the crash were never recovered.

Steve became good friends with the Lightfoots. As instructed, Nabuko Lightfoot kept her silence with Yoshima and didn't say anything. Lightfoot wasn't satisfied with the turmoil he inadvertently caused by creating doubt when identifying Simon Peters after he had lived as Steve Higgins for almost forty years. Lightfoot felt that he was responsible for his friend's unexplained questionable identify that now was troubling his thoughts of who he was and may have been formerly.

Lightfoot, with the assistance of the American Legion was able to probe the records at Tripler Hospital in the cases of Sergeant Steven Higgins and Sergeant Alonzo Anderson. Insofar as Steve Higgins was concerned, there was no explanation of what happened or what was new in the information culled from his medical records. However, Sergeant Anderson stated to his doctor that he was surprised to have made it to the hospital.

Sergeant Anderson's medical records contained some interesting information. According to Sergeant Anderson, he and a couple of others were lucky to be sitting near the back of the large transport plane. It was a clear day and suddenly the plane nosedived into the ocean. He could hear the captain yelling "Mayday" and on impact with the ocean, the plane broke into two pieces. The three who sat in the rear of the plane were catapulted into the ocean. Sergeant Anderson thought he was the most intact since he was totally conscious while his two companions seemed somewhat dazed.

There was a lot of debris all about them. Being a good swimmer, Anderson swam to his nearest companion and helped him get on a large piece of broken bench. He then swam to help the other marine who was hanging onto some floating baggage. He got his "thank you" and asked him to do him a favor. He said,

"Sergeant, I may not make it. Please take my dog tags and leather case in the event I don't get to see my wife again".

Anderson could see that the man was in a bad way and honored his request and accepted his personal belongings. Moments later, that marine disappeared. Anderson swam back to the other marine still managing to hold onto the bench. He, himself, began to feel extremely weak. He strapped the other man onto the wooden bench and also unloaded the other marine's dog tags onto the neck of the nearly unconscious marine. He managed also to slip the other marine's wallet into his jacket. He transferred the belongings he had in his mouth to the other marine because his pockets were full of other goods.

A few hours later, both men were picked up by a Coast Guard helicopter crew. The marine strapped to the wooden bench was in critical condition.

The heroic marine who saved Steve was evidently strapped on the wooden bench at the time of their rescue. He ended up in another department in Tripler hospital. Sergeant Anderson, who saved Simon Peters, lived for three weeks with complicated internal injuries. While Sergeant Anderson spoke to those investigating the crash, he forgot to mention the actions that he took regarding placing dog tags on his fellow marine while in the ocean water.

In reading a copy of that report, Lightfoot figured that the dog tags and identification papers belonging to Steve Higgins were placed in the possession of Simon Peters' nearly unconscious body. This act was instrumental in having him identified as Steve Higgins, the marine who drowned. In other words, it was a clumsy mistake that the hospital staff most likely committed at a time of a very busy period in processing overseas casualties. Lightfoot sat with Simon and upon his request explained his discovery of how his new name was established.

Nabuko originated the idea of having the three of them go to Kyoto to visit Yoshima and stay at her hotel. After considerable trepidation, Steve consented with the proviso that Yoshima not be told he was the Simon Peters that she knew. That part of the re-introduction would be left up to him and Yoshima. Arriving at the Osaka airport, Nabuko steered them towards the waiting chauffeur sent by Yoshima. The route through Kyoto was so changed with many new buildings and commercial enterprises with a western influence that the old city seemed to be a new metropolis.

When they arrived at the hotel, Yoshima was waiting. She greeted them and hugged Nabuko and Hank Lightfoot. She gazed hard at Steve Higgins and she greeted him politely. After the travelers had a rest period and dressed to be with Yoshima in her apartment, they sat on modern sofas around a cocktail table and began an evening of re-acquaintance and updating their lives from their last visit. That is, the exception was Steve who listened intently to the telling of individual stories.

When Yoshima turned to Steve, she asked if this was his first visit to Japan. He acknowledged that he was in the Korean War and had passed by and from Japan to go back to the USA. He didn't remember seeing much of Japan. Yoshima indicated that it was too bad.

She recalled the 1950's period very well. She once knew a marine Corporal who she was most fond of. He visited her at every opportunity he had. Nabuko interrupted Yoshima and asked her if she still had some of the photos she once possessed. In the lull in the conversation, Steve thought about how exquisite a lady Yoshima appeared to be. She had poise, beauty, charm and grace that was in evidence as she came back with her photo album.

Yoshima went no further than ten feet to get her photo album. Steve noticed that on top of the cabinet was a picture frame of her with Corporal Simon Peters. It was him when he was a young man. Yoshima opened her album and tearfully described the lovely memories that were forever preserved deeply within her.

She said, "Sorry, but I cry every time I open this book. You see, he died in 1954 in an airplane crash".

The evening ended on that note. For Steve, his night was sleepless. What a predicament! However, he finally began to understand his need to go forward with his life.

The next day, Steve Higgins excused himself and told his friends he had an emergency to take care of at home and left for the airport.

He was convinced that he only could be one person. He was just Steve Higgins, a high- school science teacher near retirement. He made it a point to forget the stranger who died in the air crash.

HOW TIMES CHANGE!

On leaving my neighborhood food store, I was still thinking of the short, heavy lady who I have seen there before. She is always summoning me to reach high-shelved goods for her. I have also noticed that these goods that I have helped her attain are somehow not in her cart when she checks out of the store.

I believe that this was a kind of a "hello" to me. Furthermore, she must think I am some kind of dummy in not being interested in sustaining a conversation with her. I don't think that I'm as feeble minded as she was labeling me in her mind. Insofar as my thoughts are concerned, she needs another way of making friends other than having cans of sauerkraut, diced tomatoes, French onion soup, C&H sugar, handed to her so that she can put them into her shopping cart.

Outside of the store, while I was signaling my trunk compartment of my Toyota to swing open, a lady who was parked adjacent to me had the bottom of her brown paper bag break and the heavy contents scatter about the parking spaces. Immediately I took my fresh fruit and vegetables out of my shopping bag and put them into my trunk compartment and helped pick up her canned goods and put them into the bag that I offered. The lady gratefully accepted my assistance. As soon as all her purchases were collected, she expressed her gratitude by saying,

"Thank you, good looking. We make a good team. If you should have the time, we can go across the street and find something cold to drink at Starbucks".

I looked at her wide-opened eyes in her smiling face and the appeal for this kind of sophisticated "hello" had jolting magnetism bolstering in her plotted invitation.

At the coffee place, she introduced herself as Raquel. Then quickly turned to me and asked if I would allow her to see my driver's license. I looked at her when she added,

"I'm not a cop".

I handed her my driver's license, and it appeared to me that she only took a quick glance at it. She told me,

"I gave you my correct name, and you gave me yours; therefore I pronounce you to be on the up and up. Since it is apparent that I am attracted to you, I want to know if you think my appearance is great and if you are appreciative of how I look".

I knew that I had to be quick in my response,

"Raquel, you are a great tease, and I like the fact that we are here together. You are very attractive, and I don't quite understand how you knew I would give you my shopping bag".

"Well, Terrance Newton, 5'11", eyes of brown, 177 lbs., born on January 8, 1956, I want to know more about you, so I'm wondering if I can strip away information from you that I need to know but not take ten days of coffee to have my concerns addressed.".

"I'm sure glad that I don't see any torture racks here. So go ahead and see if I'll measure up to whatever great standard I have to meet".

"First, tell me there's nothing going on between you and that short, fat lady I saw you with in the grocery store".

"Listen, I just kind of know what she eats. Otherwise, I only know she needs help beyond reaching the top shelves at the food market".

"Ok, this is the test I am going to give you. Here is a book of Post-its and a pen that you can use to help track my multiple choice exam. Ready?

Tell me which of the following ladies you would have wanted to meet and keep as a good friend?

    A. John of Arc
    B. Madame Bovary
    C. Marie Terese, Queen of Austria
    D. Marie Antoinette
    E. Cleopatra
    F. Mary Magdalene"

"I select Marie Terese. She was a wonderful, well- adjusted elderly lady. I have issues with A, B, D, E, and F".

"I like your thinking. I agree that you would think Marie Antoinette was not a good choice because she was too sheltered from reality and that fact caused her to wrongfully lose her head in order that the masses could have their day.

The second question is, which of these historical persons do you think you are closest to you in talent?

    A. Robert E Lee
    B. Billy Budd
    C. Robert Burns
    D. Oscar Wilde
    E. Somerset Maugham
    F. None of them".

"That's easy. I only create the food I eat, the travels I take, and the excuses I give myself for not exercising. I only write when I am controlled by war because I cannot use the telephone. "F" is the answer I have no trouble embracing.

Raquel, when can I give you my exam"?

"First, please get me a refill on this ice coffee, and, then I'll tell you about me and why this is fun for me. Thanks for the coffee. Let me even the score because I didn't show you my driver's license. My full name is Raquel McCormick. I was born with that name and no one has changed it with a ring of any kind. The year that I had my first cry was on December 21 of 1954. I've retained my college weight and my height. What you see is that I'm not missing any of my estrogen. I'm assertive and scare the bejesus out of most people, especially males….. How are you doing"?

"Raquel McCormick, do you have a gun at home?"

"No".

"Good. Then, you can be as assertive as you want. Here is your Post-it tablet and pen.

Please answer the questions of my quiz:

Give me the order about which chores you dislike the most:

- A. Making the bed
- B. Washing, folding, and ironing clothes
- C. Vacuuming the house on a regular basis
- D. Washing dishes, pots, and pans
- E. Cleaning the bathroom
- F. Mopping the floors
- G. Keeping all cabinets and drawers organized
- H. All of the above".

She responded by saying,

"You are a clever rascal."

She put the Post-it pads aside and indicated that her memory was excellent.

"I hope you have no need to ever find out how well I retain things. My memory is as good as it gets; therefore, this is how my order goes: E, F, B, G, A, C, and D. Forget H unless you are providing me maids".

"No maids. What else?" She asked.

As I prepared to give her this multiple-choice quiz, I had in mind that it was she that started our conversation by telling me that the more normal ten meetings be pared down to this occasion.

Which of the following would you agree to do?

    A. Sleeping with me tonight at my place.
    B. Sleeping with me tonight after a nice dinner at a hotel.
    C. Sleeping with me tomorrow and the next day at a Russian River cabin that a friend of mine lets me use.
    D. Sleeping with me starting tonight for as long as you want.
    E. None of the above."

"Forget E. There's only one thing that seems Ok for me. That's D. It's a go until I or you say "No, go".

"Raquel McCormick, you may love to change your last name in time".

"A big diamond ring has to pop out from a jewelry box in order to change my mind and name. It may be time to do that. How much money do you have in your savings and checking accounts?"

In an hour and twenty minutes, Raquel and Terry left the coffee shop to cross the street to get to their cars. Their arms hooked. Both were happy.

In viewing their skipping across the street, it could almost be imagined that an older Dorothy and the Scarecrow were prancing down the yellow brick road to see the Wizard.

GRANDMOTHER'S
VISUALIZATIONS

The greatest part of the day was at dusk. The darkness brought out a quieter time that dissipated the energy which light stimulates on what is living.

After a day on the boat, Grandpa and his two grand kids were ready for grandmother to set the stage for the evening conversation. As far as could be recalled, Grandmother was always the evening's event coordinator. Gathering the family for talking to each other was a tradition because of her deep belief that a family hour was a way to talk about life. This was a family affair ritual that everybody loved. Essentially, it was asking "What do you think about this subject or situation"? One or two topics were suggested for each to discuss at the evening's meeting. The children liked expressing their own views and, with the help of family questions, they were able to explain their own thoughts at the family circle.

The grandkids also liked to listen to the elders because in just the span of three generations much had happened and changed in their environment. Grandparents' memories were long and offered many surprises for the youngsters. In the 60 years of time, difference between the represented persons' significant history was shared and bridged.

"Tonight, let's talk about what you think was the most important invention in the twentieth century"?

"Can I go first" asked fifteen-year-old Sebastian? "I think the most important invention was that of the automobile. Not only did it result in many factories making cars and parts but it also gave employment to thousands of people. It lead to our nation having international trade, to import rubber, oil, gasoline, and leather. Roads and highways were necessary to build. Houses had to be modified to be built with garages. When I'm sixteen, I can start driving. I'll drive myself to college. I'll be freer".

"That makes sense" said Grandma looking at Grandpa. Honey, it looks like the boys are going first. So, please take your turn".

"For me, anesthesia is very high up on my list of great inventions. The wounds I received in the war, my heart surgery and having tooth implants without enduring excruciating pain is the modern miracle. Before there was anesthesia, the folks who broke limbs, needed surgery or sustained injuries, without the help of today's wonder drugs, were tantamount to torture".

Lucy was almost thirteen years old. Her pre-consciousness was admired by her grandmother, who said,

"Lucy, it's your turn".

"My mother explained to me the importance of the Nineteenth Amendment. She said that the uniqueness of our USA Constitution was that it was adaptable for making later changes to the document that was ratified in 1787. I say that the Nineteenth Amendment gave me, as a woman, the full rights that all U.S. Citizens have. I told my teacher what my Mom told me, and she agreed with us. That's how my Mom's thinks and it's my thinking, too. Is that okay, Grandma"?

"That's well stated, Lucy. So far, everyone is hitting the nail on the head. Everyone's ideas are terrific. I'm going to have a time staying on the high plane that has been established this evening. None the less, I am very passionate about what I miss most and what has disappointedly changed in the last two generations.

But I give a big "thank you" for TV not being invented when I was little and a teenager. Nothing since has compared with radio drama series. Radio programs taught me how to listen and stirred my imagination to create my own visualization of characters who were on the radio. My ears talked to my brain. My eyes functioned when I learned to build on what radio programs taught me. Later, I learned to transfer my own visualization to books. Radio was the catalyst which first allowed me to give color to what my mind only heard verbally.

During the period in my life when I was being formally schooled, I was informally educated by the radio programs which I listened to. My mind had to expand the limitations that radio had built in for me to edit. I had to do my own imagining and staging throughout every radio program. That was such good training for me. The stories on the radio made me a participant in the story plots. In most cases, I had to retain where a program left off to be resumed a day or week later. I had to think about resuming what I had previously put into play in those broadcast episodes.

Mystery programs such as "The Shadow", "The Whistler" were not only exciting, they were champions in outwitting the evil characters who popped up. By being aware that evil exists but would be expeditiously dealt with, gave our generation great comfort. We felt "safer" when we were backed up by the Shadow. I have to tell you that radio stories as well as books stimulated my brain on a continuous basis. I'm so glad that radio was my companion when I was growing up. What it did for me could not have been done by TV because TV stories do the work of defining and detailing for us the characters in their staged setting. What is transmitted by television or a movie, does not leave it up to the individual person to create one's own images. The brain is less involved when hearing is accompanied by seeing as in TV. Radio made you invoke the seeing".

That is all that was said on the night that the kids had to return home.

At Christmas, Grandpa and I went to our son's home. The kids were all excited.

"Grandpa and Grandma, we have presents for you. You have to open them." said Lucy. "We opened ours this morning."

Grandpa was handed the biggest package that was addressed to both grandparents. When he opened it, he found a Bose radio/ CD player. The smaller package that Grandma opened had CD's containing many episodes of the programs: I Love a Mystery; The Shadow; The Whistler; Stella Dallas; Jack Benny; The Saint; Fibber McGee and Molly; and books: The Caine Mutiny, Billy Budd; Robinson Crusoe; Complete Stories of Edgar Allen Poe, and Complete Stories of Sir Arthur Conan Doyle and many episodes of Perry Mason.

Dad had to change a lot of cassettes into CDs so you could remember what has not completely disappeared.

"Grandma, we'll get you more next summer so we can talk about how you visualized these dramas or comedies. Ok?

Oh….. Grandma….. don't cry."

FRIENDS CHANGE

Jessie Lynch and Maurice Shay were good friends. They were not always good for or to each other. They had known each other since they attended a middle school that politicians kept renaming every three or four years. They had graduated from high school and baffled their parents by telling them they didn't have a clue what they could do to make a living.

Mrs. Irma Lynch told her son, Jessie, he had less than a year to make enough money so he could leave their abode. She was blunt in telling Jessie to get on some path that led somewhere. Mr. Patrick Shay, Maurice's father, told his son that he himself had been on his own from the time he was fourteen. He added that he had been married and supporting his industrious wife at nineteen, just a year more than his son's current age. Addressing Maurice, he asked,

"How the hell can you go to school for eighteen years and know nothing about making a living"?

When Jessie heard about a job at a shoe store, his mother said,

"That's better than you staying around the house all day and thinking the world is unfair. Your own thoughts about how you qualify yourself do not matter. It's what the job market feeds back to you that should have your attention. Real jobs require more learning and a lot of dedication. The right job has to be a high priority in life".

After Jessie took the job at the shoe store, he discovered that he liked being busy. Three weeks later, Maurice ended up taking a job at the same shoe store when his friend told him of the vacancy which occurred there. Mr. Shay was not impressed that his son was taking a job with what he termed as another "no-gooder".

"How was he to learn anything from another guy who had yet to find himself"?

There was legitimate concern in both of the young men's households because their entry jobs seemed to be like threading water and going no place. On the other hand, the jobs would be temporary and allow the youngsters to earn money while learning a work routine.

The retailing of shoes was different in that most customers were not ready to zero on a particular style and had to try an assortment of styles to see how they looked on them. Putting shoes into individual boxes and shelving them was not as much fun as making sales. Inventory night was boring because the styles and sizes that had been sold needed to be re-ordered.

In six months' time, the manager of the store left and Jessie took his place. His promotion meant that in addition to his salary he would make eight percent commission of total store sales. Maurice didn't think it right that Jessie should get dollars for sales he made. That issue only lasted three weeks because Maurice decided to quit. He took a job driving a milk truck and delivering milk to markets and households. He now made about what Jessie was netting at the shoe store.

Before the year that Mrs. Lynch had established for Jessie to move out, Jessie found a furnished apartment that he rented. Jessie and Maurice continued their established routine of stopping in at Fred's Bar every Friday before going home. There, they would decide to go to the movies, to eat out, go bowling or play pool. The apartment Jessie rented sounded to Maurice like a place he wanted to share with his buddy. Jessie agreed, and the cost of the rent and utilities was shared.

At first, inviting girls to the apartment was not a problem. It became a problem because Jessie's mother visited their rented apartment and found evidence that some hanky-panky activities had taken place.

"You dopes", said Mrs. Lynch. "Don't you know that any girl that can stay out all night is totally irresponsible and a tramp. Most likely, she's no good and wants to compromise you".

The pot boiled over when it was discovered that Maurice was doing more than delivering milk to Mrs. Washington's household.

One day, the call came from a hospital that Maurice was seriously hurt and had to be transported home from the emergency room. Jessie took a cab and saw his buddy all bandaged up. Mrs. Washington was at the emergency room crying and fearing the consequences of her husband being put in jail for assaulting Maurice. How was Mrs. Washington going to continue to live with her mate knowing his tendencies for violence? It all ended with a "sorry" rendered by Maurice. He told Mrs. Washington,

"It's now a problem for you and Mr. Washington to resolve. We're through. I'm not delivering any more milk to nobody"!

"We should say you're not "echoed the milk company executive that fired him".

When Maurice had enough of Mrs. Lynch's Chicken soup, he began reading the classified ads that listed job opportunities. He couldn't seem to be interested in anything that was listed. His only recourse was to ask to go back to selling shoes so he could pay his half of the rent. On Friday night, both friends went to their neighborhood watering hole and sat down in their well-worn booth to figure how they would spend the rest of the evening. Gloria Aguirre, a well-known patron of Fred's Bar who had been in high school with Jessie and Maurice, came over and invited herself to join whatever conversation was at hand. She wisely didn't make any remarks about the yellow skin circling Maurice's eyes – a marker from his meeting with Mr. Washington. Gloria asked,

"What are you fellows doing tonight"?

Both of them perked up.

"Do you have any ideas? We were just considering going to take in one of the movies that has its first showing today".

Gloria offered her suggestion.

"Sally Gorman is having a party for Mikey and Aaron, who are moving to Pittsburgh. Aaron is from there and has a job with a waste management outfit".

"Do you think we can just barge in? We don't even know Aaron".

"Hey, Sally and I are like sisters. She has invited me and anyone I wish to bring".

We walked the two blocks to Sally's house and could sense by the loudness of the music playing that there could be complaints from neighbors. When we arrived, there was standing-room-only at the entrance and fast pace dancing in an adjoining room. The non-alcoholic beverages available at the open bar were being spiked with alcohol by a number of individuals who had their own flasks.

Jessie gave Gloria the excuse that he was tired because he could gauge the possibility for problems and felt that Maurice was monopolizing Gloria. He felt awkward and left out. It was too late for a movie, so he went home. Three hours later, he heard the sirens. He accurately guessed where the police cars were headed. He congratulated himself for leaving the party.

Hours later, his telephone rang.

"Jessie, I'm in jail. The cops are going to hold me here until tomorrow. You'll have to do the shoe store all by yourself".

"What happened"?

"I punched out a guy who fell through the front room window and had to be hospitalized".

"Why the hell did you fight"?

"The guy bit Gloria hard on her left boob. I just couldn't stand there and do nothing".

"Listen Mo, you are not a reliable worker. You're always in or near trouble. What now"?

""Don't worry. Gloria is going to get me a lawyer. She is having photos of where she was bitten and is arranging to sue the s.o.b. That evidence will establish my provocation. Sally just wants someone to pay for her window and broken furniture – maybe it's going to be as high as five hundred dollars".

Saturday was a busy day at the shoe store. Jessie worked in shirt sleeves. He was perspiring profusely and, at the end of the day, about sixty or more shoe boxes and shoes were strewn throughout the store. What to do? He didn't have the energy to put the shoes into their correct boxes, to shelve them, and vacuum, etc. Jessie went to Fred's Bar since he knew he could get a bowl of chili beans, crackers and a beer for $3.50 and walk to his house to shower and stretch out to relax.

While Jessie was consuming his chili, Gloria came over and told Jessie that Mo was being kept in jail until Monday because the guy that went through the window also lost two front teeth and had filed a complaint against him. Jessie looked at Gloria and said,

"Gloria, I don't care". Then, he had an idea.

"Gloria, what kind of a job do you have"?

"I work at McGregor's Textiles. I'm an inspector, as well as do minor repair of machinery when it breaks down".

"How much do you make a week"?

"Why"?

"Because I need someone to help me at the shoe store. Mo is not reliable. I'll pay you one hundred ten dollars for a six day week. Is that good enough"?

"Yes, you're on".

"Can you can help me straighten out the mess I made today at the shoe store"?

"Yes, let's do it".

Gloria didn't come to work until next Thursday since she needed to give the manager a few days to find a replacement for her. When she started at the shoe store, Jessie found her to be a very good worker. He kept his lazy friend Mo on through Saturday. He paid Mo an extra week, and all three went to Fred's Bar to wish Mo luck in his next job. Jessie was beginning to have a good deal of an admiring interest for Gloria from afar. However, that next Friday, Mo was there to walk her home. Jessie did notice that on the following Friday when Mo asked Gloria to go to dinner with him, she excused herself. She indicated that she had to stay home to wash clothes, to go food shopping, and to clean house. Maybe Mo was not going to interfere with his chance of courting Gloria when the opportunity presented itself.

When Jessie asked Mo to please find another place to live, he told Jessie that he couldn't move out of their apartment because he couldn't meet the rent at another apartment. When he called home, his father didn't want him to return because he feared he would take advantage of him and not meet his full obligations.

Gloria worked selling shoes with flourish. She was a bona fide asset because she was very direct with female customers about fit and how the shoes looked on them. She had the knack of how to shift them to a style that was appropriate for their expressed need. The only problem Jessie had was that Mo continued to think that Gloria was his girlfriend. That fact told Jessie that he couldn't try to get in the way of his friend's intentions. He felt that he had to respect their courtship. Mo was a good looking guy and Gloria seemed more attractive now than when she was at school.

One day, Gloria entered the shoe store with a folder and told Jessie that she had to be away for a few hours because she had a court hearing. She had sued the guy who bit her for assault, sexual harassment, and because she was humiliated publicly. She opened her folder and Jessie saw that she had a dated photograph of her left breast. She picked up the photograph and said,

"See, how much damage that animal did? Luckily, I'm back to normal now".

Jessie did not know what to say after seeing a photograph of her breast, so he just told her "good luck at court".

On her return to work, she skipped into the store and, without warning, kissed Jessie. Jessie turned red. She then skipped away and went to work with the next customer who entered the store. Afterwards, Jessie learned that, aside from the medical costs which Gloria had incurred, she received a verdict that the young man who bit her was obligated to pay her seventy thousand dollars within a five year time frame. Before the day ended, Mo presented himself and wanted to privately celebrate her court victory. Jessie was left out of whatever celebration was to be had.

Mo finally landed a part time job at Fred's Bar. Gloria thought that was a start, but she knew that they couldn't count on being serious yet about a future together. As time went on, Jessie wanted Mo to move from the apartment. He succeeded when Fred discovered that Mo had stolen a sizeable sum of money from the Bar's safe. He prosecuted Mo, and the result was that Maurice Shay was sent to the penitentiary for two years. Gloria was crushed. She was embarrassed. Since she had money coming in as a result of the ruling of the court, she thanked Jessie and parted to an unknown place after she hugged him and whispered that he remained her best friend.

Mo escaped from jail and was apprehended two days later. He returned to jail. A year later, Jessie heard that Gloria had married a guy who worked for the utility company. Jessie was promoted to the headquarters for the one hundred thirty-five shoe store company. He was now an assistant general manager. Nothing of significance happened until forty years later.

Now that Jessie had attained the title of Chairman or General Manager, he was recognized as being an important person in the community. Charities and non- profits had him down as a person to tap in assisting them to remain in business. He seemed to be in high demand to speak and chair drives to raise funds for good causes. One day, one of the non-profit ladies came to see him at his downtown office. She said,

"Hello, Jessie. We were in high school together. I was Sally Gorman then. My married name is Sally Finklestein".

She was not there to ask for money. She was there to request that Jessie come to their fortieth high school class reunion. Everyone in their class wanted to see him.

The day prior to attending the high school reunion, he walked from work to his house. On his walk, he saw a guy collecting aluminum beverage cans from the garbage can across the street. It was Maurice. He turned his head and asked himself what he had ever seen in that guy. Long ago, he had told Mo not to come around to see him. He wanted nothing to do with a drug addict.

The next day, he went to the class reunion. He took the first seat at one of the tables. He was pinning on his name tag when he heard a familiar voice say,

"Here, let me help you".

It was Gloria. She looked great! As he stared at her, she hugged him and whispered,

"I have missed you so. Weren't we foolish for never dating"?

In that kind of quick moment that women can share with each other, Gloria caught Sally Finklestein's wink.

Jessie was overwhelmed. Here he was in a wrong place to display or give voice to his acute feelings. He agreed that he was wrong in never ever voicing how he wanted to know her better. Jessie came to his senses.

"Are you married"?

"No, Butch died thirteen years ago. He was electrocuted."

"Do you have family in town"?

"I'm all alone and meeting you is a dream come true for me. Are you married"?

"No, I could never find anyone as wonderful as you".

The school reunion was a bore to both of them. They thought the school reunion would never end, so they could resume looking into each other's eyes. How splendid it felt to be in each other's arms. Each knew that they belonged together. At age fifty-five, life was zooming into the happiest ending.

MARKERS

The small mule deer jumped out from behind the sage brush bush, and Miles swerved his dune buggy to avoid hitting it. The dune buggy that was going full speed hit a deep rut and rolled over several times.

When the dust settled, Miles Shov could see and feel his bent right ankle swelling. He un-harnessed himself to escape from what was left of his destroyed dune buggy. His body was intact except for a broken or sprained ankle and a deep scratch on his arm. The dune buggy appeared as if it had run over a land mine.

Miles sat down and with a great deal of pain removed his shoe from his right foot. His foot seemed to be making itself into a ball. Putting his weight upon his left foot and pulling himself on the metal bars of his trashed dune buggy and managed to stand up. His thoughts started to come together and the situation seemed bleak. The desert was hot and his supply of water had spilled. His emergency kit was buried in his backpack. He didn't think he could strap his backpack on because he couldn't bear additional weight.

Miles tried to pry loose a piece of the dune buggy's superstructure but he quickly gave up because everything was hot and bent. There was nothing in the vicinity that he could use as a cane or crutch. He tore his shirt into strips to wrap them around his ankle. He then started his walk. Miles had little fear of not surviving because other dune buggy enthusiasts and human desert rats wandered around in that barren, sandy area.

The day was darkening when he saw movement behind the sage brush. Then he saw that a small deer was walking and falling and dragging itself. A closer look told him it had been shot. Moments later he saw a man pointing a rifle and yelling "Stand Clear". The man took his kill shot and the small animal flattened on the sand.

"There will be a late dinner tonight", rasped a small dark man in camouflaged shirt and trousers. He wore a torn Mexican straw-woven hat. He looked carefully at Miles and laughed,

"That your pile of junk down yonder? Look at you. You're developing a club foot late in life. Stand your ground until I get you a walking stick to hold onto".

The bearded stranger left carrying the dead deer around his shoulders. Miles felt it was his lucky day because he was being rescued from his immediate plight. In minutes, the old timer returned driving a World War II jeep that was re-wired together and had a make-shift roof added.

"Well, Dune Buggy, what did they called you after you were placed in the arms of your mother"?

"My name is Miles Shov".

"Miles Shov, put it there"!

Then the old timer put out his big hand that was as hard as a new catcher's mitt. He stated his name was Cahuama Rios.

"I won't be offended if you call me C-R".

C-R handed Miles a wooden staff for him to use to support the right side of his body.

"Listen, Miles, I can take you back where you came from but not today because I'm "chowing" down on this dead beast tonight. You're invited if you choose to climb onto Annie and help me dress down and cook this baby that strayed from its greener pastures".

Miles didn't want to stay by himself and kindly accepted C-R's casually rendered invitation to go with him. Both climbed into Annie and off they left in a cloud of dust a la Lone Ranger on his horse, Silver. The reality was that C-R could be more like the Indian scout-companion than the Lone Ranger.

They didn't travel far before they arrived at a small trailer with adjacent tents. There was a circular rock fireplace on which an iron pot hung from rebar rods. Sitting near the fireplace was an old woman who looked like she might be an American Indian.

"That's Socorro, Trejo's wife. They are my dear friends, and they make life more restful and engaging for me".

As Trejo appeared with a cache of seaweed and edible cacti, Miles' dune buggy accident and his swollen ankle were explained to Socorro. Trejo and Socorro manipulated their large knives with such skill that the deer was dressed and cut into venison chunks within minutes. Drinks which contained alcohol were passed around by C-R while supper was being readied. Miles liked the group. He felt that he fit into their circle.

While supper cooked, Socorro wrapped some kind of seaweed around Miles' swollen ankle and, in time, the pain began to diminish. Socorro asked Miles if he was in a late stage of life.

"No, I'm only sixty-three years old".

Miles could tell that for some reason, he was not communicating. Therefore, Miles opened and closed his fingers on both hands six times and added three fingers to illustrate the years he had lived.

C-R laughed at the way Miles and Socorro stared at each other. C-R explained that in Socorro's life a marker wasn't set at the beginning of her life. Therefore, years were not part of her understanding. He told Miles that years were a European regulation made in order for there to be a marker for everybody at birth. Furthermore, he added,

"Don't you know that without regulations, you have to make up your own way of measuring everything? Thoroughbred horse owners made a regulation that all of their race horses must have their birth registered on January 1st of the year in which they were born. Trejo tells the age of his animals by looking at the length of their teeth. Miles, I'll tell you how Socorro and I see things when there are no markers".

"I'd like to hear it. I never probed the topic of age because I always believed it was set by world consensus. I always thought that the distance from one's birth date established age in days, as in a 365.25 day year".

"I understand all that but Socorro and Trejo believe they are in a bubble. They see time as divided into stages, such as (1) being young, (2) having primetime and (3) being old. Being young is the time when persons are not yet who they will become. Primetime is when sexual energy and traditions are packaged to give them their own identity. Old age is when they understand their prime life's duties, experiences, and learn to pace existence. They have learned this from nature.

Plants and other animals add treasure to life. Any mistakes, injuries, sickness, or inattention shortens or ends survival. In their bubble, it is okay to establish personal markers. We, I am including myself, are not yet at a point that we can understand all the markers that governments want us to live by. We who are away from the nonsensical scope of Madison Avenue in New York can adhere to our mutual agreements. Furthermore, we believe that this nation's advantages and disadvantages come from the fact that, in earlier years, the first main bubble was bumped by smaller bubbles. Some bubbles merged and made the big bubble even bigger. Not all bubbles burst. They remain intact and left to shrink slowly. The thought is that they have not been assimilated into the big bubble. We exist in a very tiny bubble.

Markers are now governed with the vested laws of the main bubble. Markers in lesser bubbles are left to develop uniquely. And Miles.....our bubbles are similar to what you understand to be ethnic enclaves. The point is that here you have us not knowing what day it is. What difference does it make for us to know if it's Tuesday or Wednesday? In our little bubble, we have to have food and drink, sleep, work, and deal with our bodily needs, without regard to a time scheduled marker. It is interesting that our children have forsaken our bubble and want to live in the big bubble with its regulations. Hopefully, they are as happy as we are."

C-R stood up and interrupted the conversation that could have lasted until morning. However, he said,

"We need to take care of a few things prior to turning in. We have to clean our pots, mess kits, store the venison, and get Miles ready to rest. Miles, it would also be good if you have Socorro change your dried up sea kelp with fresh wrapping of the same".

Everyone rose to do the required maintenance. A rubber mattress was filled with air for me, and I was shown to my space. My ankle hurt but I felt lucky to be in their company for the night. Before retiring for the evening, C-R told me that he would take me to the nearby town so that I could get a tow truck to get the dune buggy to a garage to determine if it could be salvaged. It was necessary to get an early start so as to prevent the dune buggy from being stripped of its tires, motor, and metal. I, too, was anxious to recover my tool box, helmet, goggles, and ownership papers.

At daylight, C-R took me to the dune buggy so that I could recover my personal property. C-R placed an orange flag on the nine-foot pole next to the dune buggy so it could be easily found by the towing service that would be sent to pick it up.

Once C-R and I entered the very town where I had left my pick-up and dune buggy trailer, C-R was about to deposit me at my pick-up and trailer and say his good-bye. He extended his hand for a good-bye when I asked him if I could camp with him and his friends for a couple more days.

I felt I needed to be schooled about how missing markers affect thinking. I wanted to ask my friends how virtue and morals are accomplished without rules. What advantages are there in living out of lock step?

With a smile, C-R said,

"Come, be our guest. Bring some whiskey so it can help add to our morsels of wisdom".

IT WAS 1970

The first time I laid eyes on him, he was holding up a commercial string mop and smelling it.

"Who is that guy"? I asked myself. I walked down the long hallway and asked the chubby, no neck guy,

"May I help you"?

"Depends, who are you"?

"I'm the Coordinator of Summer Schools".

"In that case, you certainly can help. Do you detect the smell of urine in the school hallways? It's because the janitor has mopped the floors with the same dirty mop that he uses to clean the bathroom. Look at this closet. It's decease-ridden. The custodian must be a sick man".

"Sir, who are you? Are you from the Board of Health or from some governmental agency"?

"My name is Dr. Shah. I'm the new Superintendent for the Unified School District, and your name is …".?

Since I had read in the newspaper that the district had a new Superintendent, I took the dirty mop and custodian's closet remarks seriously and introduced myself to him.

"What kind of a principal would allow these conditions"?

"Dr. Shah, the janitors do not report to the principal. They have their own department, union, and the authority to assign their workers".

"Never heard of such a ridiculous setup. This should be changed".

"Do you wish to meet the summer school principal"?

"Later. I want to go to see what's taking place in the classrooms. Let's go this way".

He led the way to some isolated classrooms. We entered the large classroom in the back of the auditorium. The students were lined up ready to go to their next class.

"What class is this"? He asked the teacher

"It's a drama class".

"Why are they not working on a play"?

He then told the line of students,

"Students, take your seats".

"Wait a minute," said the Drama teacher. Who the heck are you"?

I said, "Let me introduce you to our new Superintendent of Schools, Dr. Shah".

"Ahhhh, Ohhhhh" the drama teacher uttered.

"Why are you wasting the time of these students? Why are they not working and learning something? Aren't they here to learn"?

"You see, Sir, we just finished reading "Our Town", and we are going to take up a new play tomorrow".

"Why not today? What can they learn by standing in line? How much time before the bell rings"?

"About three minutes".

"What's the next play"?

"It's "The Death of a Salesman".

"As I recall, that play entails very few roles. Shouldn't your plays have greater student involvement? How about something like "Bye, Bye, Birdie"?

At that moment, the school bell rang. The students left their seats on the way to their next class. We left with the students as he turned to me and stated,

"Let's go to the next class".

Dr. Shah went to the next class of students as the students were still coming and going. A science teacher, who I personally knew from our home school, came to the doorway to say hello. I introduced him to our new Superintendent. He vigorously stuck his hand and then froze, gulped, and quickly said,

"Let's wash our hands". He gently steered the Superintendent to the wash basin because the science teacher had just skinned a cat and had blood on his hands.

We could see the carcass of the skinned cat and the girls came in the door rendering disapproving sounds as they viewed the naked feline. The boys were more caustic and remarked that lunch was being prepared for the class.

The new Superintendent thought we should travel to the next class. It was a class in geometry I. I was introducing the new Superintendent to a newly credentialed first year teacher when she put both her hands on her groin and ran out of the classroom proclaiming that she would be right back.

The Superintendent didn't hesitate. He took over by asking what the lesson of the day was. He knew his geometry. The teacher of the class never returned. The principal of the summer school came to the classroom and was surprised to see us there. She knew me, but who was the guy teaching the class? I explained that the "teacher" with long sideburns and a not clean-shaven face was our new Superintendent. The principal whispered that the geometry teacher had reported a predicament to her. She was advised to go home.

After his teaching session, the Superintendent met the summer school principal and requested that she schedule an impromptu faculty meeting. She indicated that it would be against the district's rules because such a meeting would intrude on the teachers' duty-free lunch time.

The Superintendent said, "Let's buy them lunch".

I looked at the principal and she looked at me, and we agreed we had no such budget. I told the Superintendent that we ourselves were working in Summer School because we had families and we couldn't buy one hundred twenty-five lunches. He said,

"Don't worry. Charge it. The Central Office will pay for them".

I had never heard of such an expenditure. However, close-by we found a delicatessen which would take the school's requisition if it were signed by the new Superintendent. The box lunches arrived just in time for the voluntary 12:20 p.m. faculty meeting. The principal introduced the new head of the Unified School District to the faculty.

Dr. Shah said that there were happenings taking place in the society that we should make students aware of. Times were changing rapidly. He agreed with Alvin Toffler's views as presented in his book "Future Shock". He hoped that teachers who had not read it, would do so. In that book, the author stated that a society that was not prepared for the "information age was a society in jeopardy if it did not unlearn the old and begin to learn about the new skills that were in demand. A new paradigm had to be invoked.

The new challenge was that people in the United States had to prepare for "too much change in too short a period of time".

Also on the Superintendent's mind was what was going on in Berkeley and Oakland, California. He capsulized what Angela Davis was fighting for. Then, he discussed his own philosophical views for improving integration in the schools. He claimed that the West Coast was more likely to begin to move towards equalizing educational opportunity for all students than the East coast cities where he had been working.

The teachers gave him respect but many at the meeting didn't believe any top-down attempt for making change was a workable solution for changing the school district's curriculum. After the meeting, he met with the principal and me. He asked me how many high school students were going to graduate from Summer School. I told him the combined three summer high schools would jointly have between eight to nine hundred students. He then offered us his services as a speaker at the graduation ceremony. That was great, since we had not yet enlisted anyone to be speaking at a commencement ceremony that was still over three weeks away.

He looked at the principal and myself and said he had some requests to make. He didn't want "Pomp and Circumstance" music played at the High School graduation. He wanted the graduates to march in to the music of "The Age of Aquarius" and march out to the music of "We Shall Overcome". He shook hands with us and left.

I'll not mention what the summer school music teacher said when I conveyed the Superintendent's requested change in music for the school graduation ceremony. We gave the music teacher the necessary requisition for the new music so that he could go downtown and obtain the required sheet program needed to comply with the new way of dealing with the graduation. Apparently, Dr. Shah left town to pick up his Eastern belongings and move here in permanent residency. We counted on him to again be with us on his return from New York State on graduation day.

At the graduation class exercises, the three summer high school principals were on the auditorium stage waiting to have Dr. Shah to accompany them. He needed to be introduced to the capacity crowd of parents and students. Since he didn't appear, I announced that he had probably been delayed and might yet make it before our ceremony was over. As it turned out, Dr. Shah stood up in mid-auditorium and announced that he was ready to take his place at the podium. He indicated to the crowd that he wanted to see the students march into the auditorium. He also wanted to take advantage to speak with parents who were in the audience. He gave his speech and from that point on, everything went extremely well.

His speech was well received. He indicated that the door for graduates was half open. Learning was for a lifetime. Adapting to current changes was highly important should you want to keep relevant in the Information Age. Special skills will be needed in tomorrow's world. For those who acquire them there will be ample employment. How persons behave and how they think are keys for a successful life.

I was impressed with our new school Superintendent because he was a hands-on person. He came across as a very down in the trenches individual who wanted to improve the institutional small town flavor of our schools by preparing students for change and for acquiring problem solving skills. He was an integrationist and he verbalized his commitment to the poor and minority students. His ideas created problems. They were not supported in-house. His governance was on borrowed time.

(The story occurred in 1970, and it is factually true except for the name of the Superintendent).

OUR EARLY GIANT STEPS

Chrenshaw was teaching a lesson in his geography class and substantiating scientific theories of how the earth formed and took its place circling the sun. With brief explanation, teacher Chrenshaw summarized previous lessons concerning continental drift, atmospheric changes, development of sea life, growth of flora and fauna, formation of glaciers and how all these changing factors contribute to form our planet.

Chrenshaw's two or three forty-minute lessons were very well received by students. Most of the students had not heard or read much of what he was reviewing about the natural pre-historical events. The discovery by Dr. Mary Leaky of pre-human skeletal remains that she named "Lucy" -a four- and- a- half million year old humanoid, was the early linkage between primates to humans.

Most history classes usually do not go back to when early Homo Sapiens made enormous contributions to the people of the world. As of today, there are still current problems in pursuing subject matter that bumps against the base rock fundamentals of some contemporary religious beliefs. School boards, being politically minded, have deliberately steered away from anything which happened before the advent of the A. D. calendar.

The class Chrenshaw taught was an elective twelfth grade class for students who had interest in going on to college. Students knew that while Chrenshaw's classes were interesting, he demanded written quality homework. A student had to work hard and do some research in order to earn an A or B grade. A number of students from his class formed after-school study groups. Sometimes teachers were invited to chair these study groups in order to help resolve or explain off-shoot or tangential aspects that were not referenced in class.

Cathy Gutierrez, a bright, vivacious young student, remained after Chrenshaw's geography class and told him how stimulating his lessons had been. She and her friends wanted to have more information on what he termed "the Stone Age". She and her friends had an after school study group and they wanted to know more about the roles of women in early times. Would Chrenshaw be so kind as to attend their study group in order to help them probe why there is so little known about Stone Age women? The students wanted to review Stone Age lives and activities.

Chrenshaw reminded them that they should have their parents' permission in order to have a discussion because ancient times were far different in family life than they are today. The pre-history of early man was mostly reported by scientists rather than historians. Science addressed the evolutionary progression of human behavior in matters that affect terms of discovery rather than how modern day history is portrayed. His stipulation for attaining parent permission proved not to be a problem because all of the study group students had called home to get the okay to remain after school to learn about the Stone Age in a session with Chrenshaw.

On that very day, Chrenshaw remained in his classroom to wait for the study group students. He was somewhat surprised when sixteen students showed up. There must have been some elaborate communication between students because three study groups were in attendance. Some of the students were not even in any of his classes. Chrenshaw reviewed the reason for his being at the meeting. It was to discuss the role of women in the Stone Age at about the time Homo Sapiens evolved as a separate and unique species. He received their verifying nods that there was agreement on the topic to be reviewed.

Chrenshaw began introducing early man to the study groups by passing around some facial portraits of what some early men looked like. He explained that when speaking about mankind, he was including male and females. Everyone could contrast the difference between the well groomed persons of today with our beastly looking ancestors who still roamed the eastern hemisphere near the end of the last Ice Age.

Chrenshaw said that the development of languages resulted mostly from the necessity of being left out of the male hunting parties in order for the females to remain at camp. They labored in gathering wood for maintaining fires, filling bags made of animal hides to carry water, and in gathering edible roots, plants, and fruit. The caring of babies established maternal bonding and the need to better explain the vocal sounds to be applied to people, places and things. Vocalizing the same sound over and over named the person, place, or thing that established them with the same sound, and these sounds became a consensus and language. Pinning down those word sounds was similar to what Humpty Dumpty said: "a word is what I say it is". That's exactly how stone agers began to develop basic languages.

Applying the same sound to a person, place, or thing was an immense leap in the thinking of early man. It changed grunts and hand-signal communication to fix the tasks to be accomplished. Using word sounds to establish tasks, name things, places and persons was the outcome for language development. Women had more complex situations. They were major decision makers as to how things were to be named. When the baby said "mama", the word "mama" was innate and adopted by all mothers.

Different enclaves of early man applied their own unique sounds and, thus, other languages were formed. With some certainty, it could be deduced that the multitude of roles females performed resulted in a major way to the contribution to language development. The development of language helped man evolve at a more rapid pace.

Women were the gatherers of edible seeds of grasses. They deduced how seeds could cover the ground to give rise to a plant that rendered the same seeds that could produce their wheat, oats, rice, barley, etc. Selecting the biggest seeds produced larger, more bountiful plants and repeating this planting process was mostly a task which required detailed steps and constant patience. Moving forward, wheat and other seed based cereals resulted in the advent of agriculture. Agriculture was another great step forward. It allowed man to establish roots in areas where they could harvest their crop and could live on a harvest a long period of time. Women were instrumental in the discovery and development of edible crops in agriculture.

Once man found a way to locate himself where he could have a steady food source, a more structured life followed. It was then that man started to claim his superiority over other mammals. Since Homo Sapiens evolved with large brains and great intellect, superior creativity and problem solving and the capacity to make tools. It was brain over brawn that proved to be a deciding factor in man becoming more numerous and a builder of things.

After the time when man hunted and gathered, maintained a fire, made fist axes and weapons, stored edible plants and fruit, and promoted the development of agriculture, the domestication of animals began. It is understood that wolves commonly looked for their food where man dumped his food wastes. When man captured wolf puppies to have them at their camp sites, man discovered an animal who could warn them of predators and enemy marauders who wanted to rob and kill. The dog was the first animal domesticated. It was the animal that was taught to help man do many tasks. They stayed in the campsites of man and in time helped with the hunt and give warning when men from other clans came to plunder and to kill them.

The process of domesticating livestock animals at sites that could grow sufficient food became another great breakthrough which moved man into using animals. The animals were bred for food or used to work. The patience of women came into play in domesticating feral birds that became the fore-runners of today's chickens, ducks, geese and pigeons. The animal ancestors of other farm animals took place over centuries. Care was taken to move the herds of grazing animals from one place to another. These animals equaled economic status when in the care of men. They also established ownership and wealth. As man migrated to search and settle the African, European and Asian lands, they took their animals and skills with them. The best lands were always the places that other men wanted and fought over. These same places established rudimentary early settlements which in some cases gave rise to civilizations.

We have covered quite a lot of extremely important breakthroughs made by early man. In all of time, early female humans had very significant roles.

It was early woman who protected and nourished the young. Early males didn't always comprehend how significant the inception of families proved to be. Mankind has always been a partnership between female and male members within each tribe or clan that flourished.

Chrenshaw finally saw that he had talked for the forty minutes of time that comprise a school period. He then acknowledged that he could not keep the senior year high school students longer and suggested that they write any questions that they may have on blank paper that he passed around. He would make an effort to answer or clarify them at a meeting time that Cathy Gutierrez would schedule. The students took their time leaving his classroom. Some wanted to insure that he would be at a future group to hear what they wanted to know.

Chrenshaw saw that the questions were well thought out and would require more of him than a commitment for an additional meeting. He had twenty-two questions. Some could be grouped together to better summarize a response to their questions.

Cathy Gutierrez was the last to leave. She handed him her paper with her questions. Chrenshaw saw that she was interested in the kinds of relationships and feelings that existed in early man. Did love exist? Did faith exist? Chrenshaw determined that he had a lot more reading and learning to do before he was challenged by the students to be more specific.

As always, Chrenshaw was learning a lot by communicating with students. He loved the fact that he wasn't going home without tasks presented by the study group questions.

Now, he needed to do some research. He couldn't wait for the next student meeting. His realization was that he, himself, needed to do more. This gave him a feeling of great satisfaction.

ABOUT THE AUTHOR

Carlos V. Cornejo is a native of San Francisco, California, and now a resident of Redwood City, California. He is a family man with adult children and growing grandchildren. He is a retired school superintendent from San Francisco's school district. He still retains his love for teaching and interacting with others of all ages. After military service and also traveling much of the world, he now spends his time puttering in the garden, overseeing his small vegetable garden and potted plants. He enjoys reading, movies, and the cultural events that are scheduled in the Bay Area. He loves to write for your amusement and his.

www.ingramcontent.com/pod-product-compliance
Lightning Source LLC
Chambersburg PA
CBHW030435290526
45786CB00001B/293